CU00822124

Landscapes of
JERSEY

a countryside guide

Geoff Daniel

SUNFLOWER
BOOKS

For Rik, with love

First published 1994 by
Sunflower Books
12 Kendrick Mews
London SW7 3HG, UK

ISBN 0-948513-85-3

Rozel woods (Walk 9 and Picnic 9)

Important note to the reader

I have tried to ensure that the descriptions and maps in this book are error-free at press date. The book will be updated, where necessary, whenever future printings permit. It will be very helpful for me to receive your comments (sent in care of the publishers, please) for the updating of future printings. I also rely on those who use this book — especially walkers — to use their common sense as well. Natural hazards are few on Jersey, but use good judgement when walking on cliff-tops in windy conditions, and allow plenty of time when exploring sea-caves or beaches at low tide. The rising Jersey tide flows very quickly and can trap the unwary. Jersey does *not* have an extensive public footpath network: some tracks may look public, but are in fact on private land. I believe that all the walks in this book are on public roads, tracks and paths, but if you discover otherwise, please respect the wishes of the landowner. Abiding by the country code (page 23) is wise in any event.

Cover: The Pinnacle (Walk 6 and Picnic 6)

A catalogue record for this book is available from the British Library.

Photographs by the author, with the exception of pages 2, 10, 11, 16, 18, 20, 33, 39, 40, 41, 49, 50, 51 and 59 (John Seccombe) and page 36 (top), which is reproduced by kind permission of the Pallot Heritage Steam Museum.

Maps based upon the 1:25,000 map prepared by the Ordnance Survey for the Island Development Committee (1981), reproduced with the permission of the IDC. Crown/IDC copyright reserved. The maps have been updated to reflect important changes up to 1993.

Printed and bound in Great Britain by Brightsea Press, Exeter

6 5 4 3

 # Contents

Preface	4
Acknowledgements; Books	6
Getting about	7
Picnicking	9
Touring	12
THE WAY WEST	14
St Helier • St Aubin • Noirmont • La Corbière • L'Etacq • Grosnez • La Grève de Lecq • Devil's Hole • German Underground Military Hospital • St Lawrence • Millbrook • St Helier	
THE EAST END	18
St Helier • Sion • Pallot Steam Museum • (Bouley Bay) • Jersey Zoo • Rozel • St Catherine's Bay • Mont Orgueil • La Hougue Bie • La Rocque • Green Island • St Helier	
Walking	22
Where to stay	22
Weather	22
What to take	23
A country code for walkers and motorists	23
Waymarking and maps	24

THE WALKS
The walks in the book are arranged starting with coastal walks running clockwise round the island from St Helier and concluding with three inland walks. The symbol ➡ indicates short circular walks which are especially suitable for motorists.

1 St Helier heritage ➡	25
2 St Brelade and Portelet Common ➡	29
3 Noirmont, Jersey Village and Portelet Bay ➡	32
4 The Corbière walk	35
5 Le Val de la Mare (Short walk ➡)	37
6 The Pinnacle ➡	40
7 The north coast	42
8 Sorel and La Vallée des Mouriers ➡	45
9 Round St Martin's and Rozel	46
10 A short stroll around Flicquet ➡	50
11 St Catherine's to Gorey	52
12 Green Island to Gorey Bay	54
13 The German Underground Military Hospital	56
14 Gorey village and Queen's Valley ➡	58
15 La Hougue Bie (Short walk ➡)	60

Buses and inter-island transport	62
St Helier town plan	25
Index	64
Island touring map	*inside back cover*

❀ Preface

Jersey feels much larger than only 45 square miles, if you invest in it a little of your time and curiosity.

For the walker, Jersey expands with every step, for there is so much visual enjoyment and so much history to stir the imagination. Each bay, each stretch of cliff-top has a story to tell ... and each mile of country lane whispers secrets of its own.

To the motorist, a distance on paper means very little when translated to miles or kilometres per hour on this island, for whichever route is planned, there will be many a reason to stop and enjoy scenery, watering hole, or man-made attraction.

The picnicker is spoiled for choice of sites, whether opting for an official site with barbecue facilities or simply settling for a quiet spot along a walk route.

Landscapes of Jersey has been written for countryside enthusiasts and is divided into three main sections: picnics, car tours and walks. You will not find details of restaurants, hotels, shop opening hours, or other conventional guide book information here: these subjects are amply covered in a free guide given to all visitors to Jersey when they arrive at the port or airport. Instead, I've concentrated on giving clear instructions for the car tours and walks, with some of my personal observations that may add interest to your exploration.

Whether you are a walker or motorist, or simply taking a family holiday, you are assured of a warm Jersey welcome and if not a guarantee, then at least a fair chance of good weather. The Gulf Stream washes all the Channel Islands, and Jersey in particular has an excellent sunshine record, well above the UK average. Jersey's climate has been compared with that of southern Cornwall but drier and warmer. Even in winter, frosts are rare and snow even rarer. No matter what season it is, photographers will appreciate the quality of light in Jersey on any clear day.

Jersey's past
Invasion in one form or another has been a key factor in Jersey's history for a thousand years ...

In the 9th century Viking raiders plundered all the

Chusan palm (Trachycarpus fortunei) seen during Walk 4 to Corbière. Palm trees come as no surprise: Jersey's climate has been compared with that of southern Cornwall, but even warmer.

Channel Islands, regarding them as a bonus on pillaging voyages to Britain and France.

Between the 13th and 15th centuries, France repeatedly tried to regain control of what was once theirs, for the islands were (and still are) part of the Duchy of Normandy. The then Duke of Normandy, King John, relinquished the mainland duchy to France in 1204, but the Channel Islands remained faithful to the king, who rewarded them with 'enhanced liberty', a gift which accounts for the way the islands are governed today.

In the Napoleonic era, France sided with the American colonists in their fight for independence and thus declared war on Britain. This resulted in defensive towers going up around Jersey (examples which remain include the First Tower, the Archirondel Tower and the Seymour Tower off La Rocque).

Most recently, Jersey was occupied for five years during World War II by Nazi forces (see the Noirmont walk on page 32 and The German Underground Military Hospital on page 56). But oddly, though concrete bunkers and towers proliferate, they seem to add a dimension to the landscape, rather than ruin it.

Today thousands of visitors 'invade' the island every year and take their pleasure … and very welcome they are made, too.

Jersey's present

If anyone tried to invade Jersey now, the island would be defended as if it were part of the UK, but all internal affairs are managed by Jersey's own parliament, known as the States Assembly. There is a Lieutenant Governor who represents the Queen, and two law officers appointed by the Crown, but the remaining States members are elected. You could watch them debating Jersey's affairs on Tuesdays at the States Chamber in Royal Square, St Helier.

Much of what you see will be familiar to British visitors. Indeed, many Britons have settled on Jersey (not easy now, because of strict residential qualifications). However, scores of roads and streets have French names, while the Jersey accent derives from a time when the Jersey-Norman patois was more widely used than it is now. It is plain fact that for all Jersey's historical antipathy to France, the French mainland is easily visible on most days ... a mere 17 miles away.

Jersey's reputation as a financial centre is well known: some 50 major banks and finance companies have their base on the island. Income tax is very low here, and there is no VAT.

Acknowledgements

I am indebted to the following for help in researching and preparing this book:

The States of Jersey Island Development Committee and Nigel Nerac of the Planning Department, for assistance with queries;

Howard B Baker of St Helier, whose intimate knowledge of Jersey, warmly shared, was of immense value, and whose own reference map 'The German Occupation of Jersey 1940/45' is a thorough and revealing document on the island's wartime experience;

Jersey Tourism, for information, hospitality and mobility, with special thanks to Diane Needham, Karin James and Pamela Daltrey;

Mike Freeman, States of Jersey Conservation Department, for information on Jersey's natural history;

The Jersey Society (La Société Jersiaise) for use of its library;

British Channel Island Ferries;

Channel Islands Occupation Society;

Judith Rand, Denise Barkman for walk-sharing and checking;

Roger Foord of LST Ltd, for help with additional walk routes.

Books

Landscapes of Jersey is primarily a guide to countryside exploration and is intended to be used in addition to a standard guide such as *Blue Guide Channel Islands* (A & C Black) or the *Visitor's Guide to Jersey* by Sonia Hillsdon (Moorland). More specific reading might include *The Bird-watcher's Jersey* by Mike Stentiford (BBC Radio Jersey); *The German Occupation of Jersey 1940/45* (Howard B Baker); and *Jersey: Witches, Ghosts and Traditions* by Sonia Hillsdon (Jarrold).

Also of interest

Landscapes of Guernsey (with Alderney, Sark and Herm), also by Geoff Daniel (Sunflower Books, 1994).

Getting about

A **hired car** is the most practical way of exploring Jersey, though by no means the only way. The Channel Islands are, incidentally, probably the cheapest place in Europe to hire a car, and most vehicles are brand new. Hire vehicles are distinguished on the island by the prefix letter 'H' on the car's number plate (many locals are sure this stands for 'Horror'). You can also take your own car to Jersey, but not a caravan or camper van (unless it is a vehicle adapted to carry a disabled person).

To be able to hire a car, visitors must provide a valid driving licence with no endorsements for dangerous driving or drink/driving within the past five years. Drivers must be over 20 years of age, but there is no upper age limit (subject to any hire car insurance company proviso). Collision damage waiver is not compulsory but, if you do not take this option, you may be asked for a hefty deposit to cover part of the insurance excess (sometimes £500 or more), and this amount would become your responsibility in the event of damage to the car. It's up to you whether you pay the extra for CDW and peace of mind. Do take the trouble to shop around for car hire: some firms allow a useful discount provided you book with them direct rather than through an agent or a hotel.

Motor cycles, **mopeds** and **scooters** can also be hired; the wearing of crash helmets by rider and pillion passenger is compulsory.

Petrol carries much less duty than at home and therefore is also much cheaper. On the fold-out touring map and in the touring notes, I have not attempted to list the location of every filling station, because there are so many; it would be difficult to drive five miles without seeing one! (Likewise, although the touring map indicates the locations of some cafés, restaurants and attractions, it is by no means comprehensive in this respect, and you will come across many more.)

Parking places and official car parks are plentiful; many are free of charge (all parking is free of charge between 5pm and 8am). At paying parks, you cannot pay cash but must display paycards, on which you indicate date and time of arrival. These are sold in packs at garages and many shops. Even at the height of the season, it is not difficult to find somewhere to park, except in the main multi-storey car parks in St Helier. But it is usually easy to find a space in the huge Pier Road multi-storey park, only five or six minutes' walk from St Helier centre. There are also many limited-waiting parking places in St Helier, some needing a paycard, some a parking disc (the latter is often provided with a hire car). If you have brought your own car, you can purchase a parking disc at the Town Hall, Motor Traffic Office, or at garages. But there are scores of free parks all over the island where you'll need neither disc nor paycard.

There is an all-island **maximum speed restriction** of 40mph/64kph, but in many places the limit is less than this, sometimes as low as 20mph/32kph. Places and junctions where you must halt are indicated by a yellow line across the road. A single yellow line parallel with the kerb or pavement means no waiting at all (the equivalent of a double yellow line in the UK). There are many roundabouts with a 'filter in turn' system — watch out for the signs. At these, one vehicle at a time enters the roundabout from each road joining it, everyone taking their 'turn'. It can be a bit confusing when you are not used to it, but it works!

Buses operate throughout the island from a central bus and coach station at the Weighbridge, St Helier. There's a very frequent service to popular centres such as St Aubin and Gorey, but the service to more distant points is also good, and especially useful for walkers doing sections of the north coast path.

Cyclists are catered for by several cycle hire depôts, and bicycles can be hired for a day or by the week.

Taxi ranks can be found at the airport and in St Helier, and there are numerous private hire companies operating. There are set tariffs, with fares clearly shown on a meter, and with different tariffs applying to day and night hire, and on public holidays.

Coaches offering day and half-day excursions are operated by a number of companies. If you use these, watch that you don't book for two or more trips with different main destinations, but with duplication of intermediate 'attractions'.

Excursions to the other Channel Islands or day trips to France can be made by sea or air; see page 63.

❀ Picnicking

Tucking into a basket of goodies out of doors is a particular pleasure on Jersey, where there are so many suitable settings. Naturally, most beaches make good picnic bases (especially for young families), and Jersey's beaches are of excellent quality and well maintained. I have picked out some of my favourite locations; most are easily accessible by bus, as well as car or bicycle.

All the information you need to get to these picnic spots is given below, where *picnic numbers correspond to walk numbers.* Beside the picnic title you'll find a map reference: the exact location of the picnic spot is shown on this *walking map* with the symbol *P.* I also include transport details (🚌 = how to get there by bus; 🚗 = where to park), how long a walk you will have, and any other information you might find useful. Nor have I forgotten those among you who have moved out of the ham-sandwich-and-flask league into steak and sausage sizzle-ups. All picnic sites with tables (and sometimes griddles) are indicated by a ⊼ in the list below and on the touring map.

Please remember that if more than a few minutes' walking is required, you will need to wear **sensible shoes** and to take a **sunhat** (○ indicates a picnic in full sun). A plastic groundsheet also comes in handy, in case the ground is damp or prickly.

1 ELIZABETH CASTLE (touring map and St Helier plan page 25; photograph page 28) ○

🚌 by bus: 30min on foot. Bus to St Helier.
🚗 by car: up to 30min on foot. Park in St Helier.
Reached on foot by causeway at low tide from opposite the Grand Hotel (or you can ride across in one of the amphibious vehicles). *Picnic in the castle grounds (where there are plenty of benches), and visit the tiny hermitage of St Helier.*

2 BEAU PORT (map pages 30-31; photograph page 11) ○

🚌 by bus: 20min on foot. Bus 12 or 14 to St Brelade's Bay. From St Brelade's Church (see map) take the signposted footpath to the bay.
🚗 by car: 10-20min on foot. Park at the car park above Beau Port Bay, reached on narrow roads signposted from St Brelade's Church (10min on foot). Or park at St Brelade's Church and take the footpath from there to Beau Port (20min on foot).
A beautiful, unspoiled little bay, really gorgeous on a warm, clear evening. Sit on grassy banks or sand.

The extensive dunes of Les Mielles: a maze of paths and many picnic places, both official and impromptu (Picnic 5a; near Walk 5)

3 NOIRMONT (map pages 30-31; photographs pages 14-15, 34) ○

🚌 by bus: 20min on foot. Bus 12 to the Old Portelet Inn; walk up the road to Noirmont.
🚗 by car: under 5min on foot. Park at Noirmont.
Dazzling views from this striking headland which is a fitting memorial to Jersey's war dead (see notes page 34). 🅰 *nearby.*

4 LA CORBIERE (map pages 30-31; photograph page 17) ○

🚌 by bus: up to 15min on foot. Bus 12 to La Corbière.
🚗 by car: up to 15min on foot. Park at La Corbière.
Stunning views in the right light from this exposed southwest corner. Some benches at viewpoints, nice grassy spots, or you could walk across to the lighthouse, depending on the tides.

5a LE MIELLE DE MORVILLE (touring map; photograph above) 🅰

🚌 by bus: up to 5min on foot. Bus 12a to Le Mielle de Morville.
🚗 by car: up to 5min on foot. Park at Le Mielle de Morville, just off the road behind St Ouen's Bay.
Three organised picnic sites with barbecues, or scores of places in the dunes. Visit nearby Kempt Tower Information Centre for details of nature trails and the history of the whole west coast.

5b LE VAL DE LA MARE (map page 37; photograph page 38)

🚌 by bus: 30min on foot. Bus 9 to Val de la Mare car park.
🚗 by car: 30min on foot. Park at Val de la Mare car park on the A12.
Follow Walk 5 (page 37) for 15min, but turn *right*, to skirt the western arm of the reservoir for a further 15min.
Grassy slopes and convenient benches; splendid views over St Ouen's Bay. Shade from trees nearby.

6 THE PINNACLE (map on reverse of touring map; photographs page 41 and cover) ○

🚌 by bus: up to 20min on foot. Bus 12a to L'Etacq (terminus).
🚗 by car: up to 20min on foot. Park at Le Grand Etacquerel.
Follow Walk 6 from Le Grand Etacquerel (the Etacq bus terminus); see notes pages 40-41.
Magnificent setting, either from the cliff path or down in the sheltered rock 'amphitheatre'. Stout shoes essential.

7a RONEZ (map on reverse of touring map) 🅰 ○

🚗 by car: up to 5min on foot. Park at the site, on the north coast east of Ronez Quarry (well signposted opposite La Fontaine Tavern).
Three grills in two areas, one in a loop of the road (useful for parking), the other two below the road (better coastal views).

7b BOULEY BAY (map on reverse of touring map) ○

🚌 by bus: up to 20min on foot. Bus 21 to Bouley Bay.
🚗 by car: up to 20min on foot. Park on the jetty just to the west of the bay (access is via the narrow C96, north of Holy Trinity Church).
Picnic at the beach, or walk up a track to Le Jardin d'Olivet, an old battleground with superb views over the sea.

9 ROZEL WOODS (map page 47; photographs pages 2 and 20)

🚌 by bus: 10min on foot. Bus 1b (St Catherine's Bay bus) to La Mare.
🚗 by car: 10min on foot. Park at La Mare slipway (St Catherine's).
Follow Walk 9 (page 46) into the woods, past the small pond.
Benches available; good shade.

11a ARCHIRONDEL (map page 47) 🎪

🚌 by bus: up to 10min on foot. Bus 1b (St Catherine's Bay bus) to Archirondel Tower.
🚗 by car: up to 10min on foot. Park at Archirondel Tower.
Two barbecue areas lie off the B29 north of the tower. Shade nearby.

11b ANNE PORT (map page 47) 🎪 ○

🚌 by bus: under 10min on foot. Bus 1b (St Catherine's Bay bus) to the Anne Port slipway.
🚗 by car: no walking. Park at the site (B29, north of Mont Orgueil).
Fine views from this headland at the north end of the little bay. Tables, but no barbecues.

14 QUEEN'S VALLEY RESERVOIR (map page 47; photograph page 59)

🚌 by bus: 15min on foot. Bus 3a or 3c to St Saviour's Hospital.
🚗 by car: 15min on foot. Park at the St Saviour's Hospital end of the Queen's Valley Reservoir.
Follow the path along the eastern bank of the lake, until you reach the causeway. Pass it and, under 5min later, climb a couple of steps to a grassy bank with pleasant views over the lake. Shade nearby.

15 LA HOUGUE BIE (map page 60) 🎪

🚌 by bus: no walking. Bus 3a or 20 to La Hougue Bie.
🚗 by car: no walking. Park at La Hougue Bie.
Tables, benches and drinks available (but no barbecues) in the very pleasant, grassy surrounds of this prehistoric site. Much to see: medieval chapels; German bunker; geological, agricultural and railway exhibits. Ample shade.

The delightful little bay of Beau Port (Car tour 2, Walk 2 and Picnic 2)

❁ Touring ────────────

Jersey is an island roughly nine miles by five (15km by 8km), with about 450 miles of good, if sometimes narrow roads. Exploring this road network will take more time than you might imagine: not only is there is much to see and do en route, but there is an **island-wide speed limit of 40mph/64kmph** (even less in some places). And rightly so. This is not an island to be taken in a hurry. However you put together your day, it would be difficult not to enjoy it on Jersey.

Most visitors like to hire a car for their stay on the island. You can take your own car if you wish, by ferry from Poole or more quickly (and at higher cost) by the catamaran service from Weymouth. Drink-driving and seat-belt laws are similar to those in the rest of Britain and are keenly enforced, especially drink-driving laws. Visiting drivers must carry their licence with them whenever using their car. For further information on car hire and driving on the island, see page 7.

The touring notes are brief: they include little information readily available in standard guides. Instead, I concentrate on taking you to my favourite natural and man-made attractions, and I emphasise possibilities for **picnicking** and **walking**, with a good selection of circular walks for motorists (see Contents, page 3).

The pull-out touring map is designed to be held out opposite the touring notes. I hope it will prove rather easier to use while motoring than some of the free give-away maps, and it shows all the roads I would recommend for car touring. But I strongly urge you use it in tandem with the 1:25,000 OS/Island Development Committee Official Leisure Map (very similar in style to a UK Ordnance Survey map). This is inexpensive and provides a wealth of detail. Extracts from this map have been used as the basis for the walking maps.

With almost 450 miles of road to explore, a few suggestions may be useful. Imagine Jersey as a wedge-shaped piece of cheese, with the thick end to the north. You can do a circuit quite easily and take your choice of north-south routes along several picturesque valleys. Moreoever, by creating a circuit using coast road and central valley, you will see the best of Jersey. But beware: east-west tours across the middle of the island are a different matter and, unless you know the lanes intimately, you are almost certain to get lost.

I offer two main route suggestions with optional side-tracks to take in some of the more popular attractions. I need hardly say that while references to things to see and do are correct at the time of writing, changes can take place at very short notice. Businesses change hands; authorities change policies over opening hours or access; every time I've visited Jersey, I have found changes. So, if there's something I have highlighted that you would particularly like to see, do check with the Jersey Tourism office, or telephone the attraction you plan to visit, before making a special journey.

Cumulative distances are given from St Helier (see town plan, page 25). A **key to the symbols** in the notes is on the touring map.

Walk 12 near La Rocque: one of Jersey's round towers rises beside a delightfully eccentric house.

1 THE WAY WEST

St Helier • St Aubin • Noirmont • La Corbière • L'Etacq • Grosnez • La Grève de Lecq • Devil's Hole • German Underground Military Hospital • St Lawrence • Millbrook • St Helier

34mi/54km; about 2-3 hours' driving

On route: 🍴 at Noirmont, Le Mielle de Morville, L'Etacq; Picnics (see pages 9-11): (2), 3, 4, 5a, (5b), 6, (7); Walks (2), 3, 4, (5), 6, 7, (8), 13
All roads on this route are in excellent condition, but be prepared for a few hairpin bends and some very narrow lanes. Watch your speed, which is restricted to 40 mph (less in some places).

From St Helier, head out on the Esplanade following the signs to **St Aubin★** (3mi ✝🏨🏠✕🖃⊕ 🚻WC), a quieter resort area than St Helier, with a delightful harbour. Keep to the narrow harbour road out of St Aubin, then turn sharp right at The Old Court House Hotel, which used to be recognisable to *Bergerac* fans as Jim's 'local'. It's a very narrow road here, through a series of hairpin bends and then alongside the walled grounds of a country house on your left. The road is joined by the B57, where you turn left to the memorial headland of **Noirmont★** (4.5mi 🚗🍴*P*3), shown below and described in more detail on page 34. Noirmont is one of the settings for Walk 3.

Return on the B57, passing roads on your left to Portelet Common (Short walk 2-2, with a splendid view over the bay) and L'Ouaisné (🚻 WC), where Walk 2 begins. Join the A13 and turn left. Stay on the main road only briefly until, at a fork, you drop down left on

Walk 3 and Picnic 3: World War II weaponry at Noirmont, the headland memorial to Jersey's war dead. St Helier is in the distance. See also photograph page 34.

the B66 to **St Brelade's Bay**★ (7mi ♦▲▲✕⊕⬛WC). The lovely church is at the end of the road, just above the harbour shown on page 29. Behind the church, take the road signposted to Beau Port Bay and climb through more hairpin bends. You pass the road to Beau Port on your left: perhaps make a detour to look at this pretty, unspoiled cove★ (▮☎⩋*P*2; photograph page 11).

Otherwise, come to a T-junction and turn left on the B83 to reach **La Corbière**★ (9mi ☎▲▲✕⩋WC*P*4; Walk 4), one of the best-known sights on Jersey, and really spectacular if you catch it at sunset (see page 17) or when the sea is running high over the rocks in a sou' west gale! La Corbière lighthouse was the first concrete lighthouse in the British Isles, completed in 1873. Its beam, now controlled remotely, is visible for 20 miles.

Continue on the B44, then turn left on the B35. You pass a signposted path to La Sergenté, the oldest tomb on the island (11mi ⋔; Walk 4), with parking nearby. Now you're at the southern end of **St Ouen's Bay**, a glorious five-mile sweep of beach, much favoured by the surfing fraternity. Continuing north, be sure to visit the Kempt Tower Information Centre (ℹ) for full details of official picnic sites, and a good exhibition and

The Devil, to be seen (where else?) but at Devil's Hole (Walk 7)

leaflets about Jersey's wildlife and nature reserves.

Beyond Le Mielle de Morville (π; ***P***5a), come to Jersey Goldsmiths (✕), a spacious jewellery emporium with a pleasant open-air restaurant (14mi). On the opposite side of the road, the Château Plaisir complex includes the unbelievable Micro World: incredibly tiny sculptures and other works of art, so minute that each has to be viewed using a powerful magnifying glass or microscope! Near the sea wall is the Channel Islands Military Museum, housing German and Allied vehicles and memorabilia in a former Nazi bunker (**M**☕).

Turn right, pass a quarry and come to a fork. Here a right turn on the B64, followed by another right on the A12, would take you to the car park for the Val de la Mare Reservoir (***P***5b; Walk 5; photograph page 38). The main tour bears sharp *left* alongside L'Etacq Woodcraft (15.5mi; wood-carving displays, including the famous Jersey 'cabbage stalk' walking-sticks; nearby pottery and leather centre; π adjacent to the car park).

Then come to **L'Etacq★** (16.5mi 📷) and see the Crucible Folklore Museum (**M**☕) on your left. Walk 6 can start a little further along the road at Le Grand Etacquerel; it visits the magnificent rock pinnacle shown on the cover and on page 41 (***P***6). Climb the hill, then make a very sharp left turn at the top, on the B55 to **Grosnez★** (18mi ♜📷), where Walk 7 starts and Walk 6 can also start. Head off on the track to the ruined fortification and enjoy the magnificent views.

Return to the B55 and bear left, then go left again to **Plémont★** (∩📷☕WC; Walk 7), where there is an excellent beach and caves to explore at low tide, as well as Plémont Candlecraft. Return to the B55 and bear left. At about 20mi, turn sharp left on the B65 to **La Grève de Lecq★** (21mi ▲✕Π📷☕MWC), where there's another fine beach and a 19th-century barracks owned by the National Trust. A working water-wheel is incorporated into one wall of the bar at the Moulin de Lecq Inn. Walk 7 passes here, too.

Head out of La Grève de Lecq on the B40, then turn left on the B33, and left again on the C103. Pass a butterfly farm and La Mare Vineyard and come to **Devil's Hole**★ (24mi ∩ 🚙💧WC), where a steepish path leads from the parking area down to a wild sea inlet. From here you could join circular Walk 8 by following the Walk 7 coastal path for a short way (about 10min).

Now return to the B33. A left turn would take you to the picnic site at Ronez (🚗*P*7a): bear left again in front of St John's Church. The main tour bears *right* on the B33 and then left on the B26 almost immediately. Go straight over the B53. The road makes a sharp right turn en route to the Fantastic Tropical Gardens★ (26.5mi ✕), catering for families with 'country' themed areas, entertainers, children's rides, puppets, parrot shows, etc.

Continue down the valley, bearing left on the A11 at a fork. Just before the Victoria Hotel, on the right, there is a small car park near a duck pond. You can stop here briefly, to walk through a lovely bit of woodland to Le Moulin de Quetivel, a mill of 14th-century origin now owned by the National Trust (see Walk 13). From the Victoria Hotel you could follow signs to Jersey's major tourist attraction, 'The Living Legend'★ (✕💧WC). Or turn right and follow the road to the turn-off (B89) for the **German Underground Military Hospital**★ (29mi). Walk 13 starts here, and takes in both the underground hospital and 'The Living Legend' (see page 56).

From the hospital car park cross into Meadow Bank, instead of rejoining the road on which you approached. Turn left on the A10 at La Ville Emphrie and go through **St Lawrence** (31mi). Less than half a mile beyond the church, fork right (a sports field is on the right and a garage on the left). Then, almost immediately, turn sharp right on a narrow lane to pass the magnificent grounds of La Chesnée, before dropping down to the Dannemarche Reservoir. Here turn right and enjoy a lovely return down Waterworks Valley, via **Millbrook**, to **St Helier** (34mi).

Corbière lighthouse at sundown
(Picnic 4, Walk 4)

2 THE EAST END

St Helier • Sion • Pallot Steam Museum • (Bouley Bay) • Jersey Zoo • Rozel • St Catherine's Bay • Mont Orgueil • La Hougue Bie • La Rocque • Green Island • St Helier

24mi/38km; about 2 hours' driving

On route: ⊼ at St Catherine's Bay, La Hougue Bie; Picnics (see pages 9-11): (7b), 9, 11a, 11b, 14, 15; Walks 7, 9, 10, 11, 12, 14, 15

All roads are excellent but narrow in places, especially near Rozel, with sharp bends. Stick to the 40mph speed limit.

Leave St Helier by heading out on the Esplanade, following the signs for St Aubin, but get in the centre or right-hand lane by the time you approach the end of the Esplanade. You will see the Inn on the Park ahead on the right; you will turn right to pass in front of it. Look for the sign for the A9: this is the road you want. Initially you'll drive up St Aubin Road, then Cheapside. The signs will direct you to the right (you'll still be in Cheapside), then take the second left into Elizabeth Place. *Watch the signs,* and make sure you keep on the correct road; it's easy to find yourself on the A8 by mistake! Clear St Helier on the Grand Route de St Jean and come to **Sion** (3mi), where there is an old Methodist Chapel (✝ 1880) built like a temple. It is enormous in relation to the size of the village. Past the chapel, on the right, is Macpela Cemetery, where European exiles who made Jersey their home in the mid-19th century were buried.

About a quarter of a mile past the chapel, turn right into Rue de Bechet, looking out for the signs to the fascinating **Pallot Steam Museum★**. This is an extensive, if informal collection assembled over several years by Mr Pallot, a local engineer. There are steam and diesel railway engines, rolling stock and a few hundred yards of full standard gauge railway track laid out in a circuit in the field behind the museum where, if you choose the right time to visit, you can ride in a train like the one shown below. In any case, at least one item is

A 1931 steam locomotive hauling Victorian coaches on the full-size standard gauge railway at the Pallot Steam Museum

One of the gorillas from Jersey Zoo's famous colony

operating under steam at all times the museum is open. There are traction engines, rare old farm machines and other machines of all kinds ... there's even an organ room! Truly a surprising sight, tucked away in the heart of the island. Leave the museum on a minor road opposite the entrance, to join the B51, where you turn right. From Trinity Church (5mi) you could make a short detour (about 4mi return) down to Bouley Bay★ (🏔🐚💧wc*P*7b): turn left at the church and then bear sharp right when you reach the C96. Follow the zigzag road (sometimes used for hill-climb motor racing) down to the bay, which is on the north coast path (Walk 7).

The main drive continues straight ahead from Trinity Church, on the B31. At 6mi come to Gerald Durrell's famous Jersey Wildlife Preservation Trust (the **Jersey Zoo★**), which does splendid work in breeding rare species and is noted for its gorilla colony. This is a must, though it's probably best to reserve at least a whole morning or afternoon for your visit here. After passing the zoo entrance, turn left on the C93, which is a pleasant run above the coastal path along to **Rozel★** (9mi 🏔✖🐚💧wc). Rozel, where Walk 7 ends, is an attractive little seaside resort with some classy hotels and good restaurants; ideal for an away-from-it-all holiday. To join circular Walk 9 here at Rozel, see map page 47 and notes page 48.

Climb out of Rozel on the B38 and look out for the B91 on the left. Reach a minor crossroads (on the route of both Walk 9 and Walk 10) and bear right past riding stables. Beyond Les Mares and Le Villot, you join the B29. Turn left. You pass La Mare slipway, where Walk 9 begins (*P*9). Then come to **St Catherine's Bay★** and Breakwater (12mi 🚻🐚💧wc), where Walks 10 and 11 begin. There is plenty of parking space here, so why not stretch your legs on the breakwater or, for more variety of scene, try short circular Walk 10.

Then return on the B29, first coming to **Archirondel**

This pleasant spot near the entrance to Rozel woods (Picnic 9 and Walk 9) is only a few minutes' walk from a convenient parking spot at La Mare slipway.

(⏻*P*11a with ⚲) and then **Anne Port** (⏻wc*P*11b with ⚲). Take a sharp left to head into **Gorey** ('Gouray' on the large-scale walking map; 14mi ♦⌂▲✕⚑⊕⏻wc) and park by the harbour. Walk up to **Mont Orgueil Castle**★ (⬛📷); the magnificent view from here is shown on pages 52-53. Walk 11 (from St Catherine's) ends here, as does Walk 12 which has come north from Green Island. From either Anne Port or Gorey you could make an interesting diversion (signposted) to the **Dolmen de Faldouët** (⬛). See Walk 11 and map page 47.

From Gorey harbour follow signs to St Martin. Half a mile along, fork left on the B28. Short walk 14 starts at St Saviour's Hospital (15mi), at the northern end of the Queen's Valley Reservoir (*P*14, photograph page 59). Continue to **La Hougue Bie**★ (16mi ♦⬛⚲ *P*15), where Walk 15 begins (see details page 60).

From La Hougue Bie, head back the way you came. Pass

You'll encounter quiet roads like this one on this tour. Show consideration for horse riders and drive slowly, especially in the narrow lanes.

the B46 off right, but bear right on the B37, past La Hougue Grange on your left. The road bends sharp left. Follow it until you can turn sharp left to the southern end of the Queen's Valley Reservoir (this is another place where you could park and do circular Short walk 14). Keep on this narrow road to Jersey Pottery★ (17.5mi ✕WC), where you can see the whole manufacturing process.

From the pottery head right to the A3, and there bear right again, to follow the coast. Soon the coast road becomes the A4 (the A3 cuts inland and would take you to St Helier via St Clement's Church and Samares Manor). The A4 gives you a chance to look at more of the coast; the seaward views are quite amazing at low tide, when the sea can recede more than two miles, revealing treacherous reefs. Your return to St Helier will be via **La Rocque**, **Le Hocq**, and **Le Croc** (honest: look at the map!), each of which has ☕WC and some parking space permitting a break of journey for a brief look round. Walk 12 starts at **Green Island** (22mi ☕WC), just before Le Croc.

As you near St Helier, either cut through the tunnel or keep to the coast past the open-air pool. This brings you round to Pier Road. You pass the Jersey Museum★ on the left, before turning left to arrive back at the Jersey Tourism office and bus station (24mi).

❀ Walking

The walks in this book are designed to take you to the loveliest parts of Jersey on the best footpaths.

Beginners: You can do most of the walks without problems, but the less nimble might find some stretches of the north coast path too steep for your liking.

Experienced walkers: All walks should be within your capability, including the north coast. This could be achieved in a day, but I would recommend making at least two days of it, to enjoy its sights fully.

All walkers: Please follow routes as described in the notes, especially where they are off-road. If at any stage you are uncertain of the way forward, go back to your last 'sure' point and start again. Do *not* try to continue a walk which for some reason has become impassable. And *I cannot emphasise too strongly* the need for caution when exploring Jersey's beaches at low tide. *Be absolutely sure of the tide times (check the local paper, or buy the tide tables at one of the shops) and always allow plenty of time to reach a safe point.*

Where to stay

Except perhaps during July and August, accommodation should never pose a problem: Jersey has more than 500 registered hotels and guest houses (inspected and graded annually by Jersey Tourism). The Tourism office produces an excellent brochure giving details of all these premises (as well as camping sites) and operates a room-finder service (telephone 78000). There is, however, very little conventional self-catering accommodation so, if you wish to reserve an apartment, you must do so early in the year.

While most people stay around **St Helier**, you may prefer **St Aubin** to the west or **Gorey** in the east. Both are charming centres, with good public transport links to St Helier. Moreover, there are many pleasant small hotels and guest houses in fairly isolated spots along the north coast, or in the heart of the countryside.

Weather

Jersey has a summer average of 8 sunny hours a day (among the best in the British Isles), and rainfall averages 33-39 inches (80-100 cm) a year. May, June and July are generally considered the best months for a visit. August is warm, but can be thundery. March and April are often dry and sunny, and Jersey has known many an 'Indian summer' in September and October.

What to take

For much of the country walking in this book, you will need little special equipment. Some walkers find trainers adequate, but I will always recommend lightweight boots which cope with almost any conditions underfoot, which on Jersey might include long wet grass, rock pools, sand dunes, muddy tracks and tarmac roads ... all on the same walk! Below is a checklist of items you might find useful, depending on the season, the weather, and the part of the island covered by your walk:

long-sleeved shirt and long trousers	binoculars and camera
waterproof trousers and anorak	small rucksack
spare bootlaces	spare jumper, extra socks
groundsheet (picnic sit-upon)	sunhat, suncream, sunglasses
telephone numbers of taxi operators	bus timetable
whistle (if you get stuck or lost)	first aid kit

A country code for walkers and motorists

The experienced rambler is used to following a 'country code', but the tourist who rarely ventures into the countryside may unwittingly cause damage or harm animals. Be aware of the following when walking:

- **Do not light fires** except at official barbecue sites. Never allow youngsters to play with matches, and never throw cigarette ends away. Fires are a very real hazard on headlands during dry summers and are difficult to deal with because of inaccessibility.
- **Keep dogs under proper control**, and **fasten all gates after you**.
- **Keep to paths** across farmland and avoid damage to fences, hedges and walls.
- **Leave no litter**: take it away or put it in a litter bin.
- **Protect wild and cultivated plants**, and never walk over cultivated land.
- **Go carefully** on narrow country roads, and don't block them by parking carelessly.
- **Respect the countryside** and the country way of life.
- The bird life of Jersey's coastal region is very important. **Do not disturb or annoy the birds**, especially during the nesting season (spring).

Here are some other points, particularly directed to

walkers planning a lengthy ramble in any of the more remote locations:

- **Do not walk alone**, and *always* tell a responsible person where you are going and what time you expect to return. If you walk in a group, and someone is injured, others can seek help, and there will be no need for **panic in an emergency**.
- **Do not overestimate your speed**; your pace will depend on the slowest walker in the group.
- **If a walk becomes unsafe**, do not press ahead.
- **Transport** at the end of a long walk is important
- It pays dividends to carry some **warm clothing** and **extra rations**, even in summer, in case you are delayed beyond sunset.

Waymarking and maps

There are some **waymarks** or signposts on the Corbière Walk, at Les Mielles and along the north coast, but few exist elsewhere, because Jersey does not have an extensive system of public footpaths. Privacy is a cherished commodity on the island, and attempts to create long distance routes have been thwarted in the past, through landowners' reluctance to allow access.

The **walking maps** accompanying the text are reproduced on the 1:25,000 States of Jersey/Ordnance Survey Official Leisure Map, readily available on the island or from specialist map shops. (Note, however, that not all paths marked on this map still exist, whilst some that do are not shown.) Where different spellings exist for place names, we have generally used the spellings on this map, to avoid confusion. Following is a **key to the symbols** on the walking maps.

B 46	main road	P (filled)	car park (public)	⛪/⛪	church/chapel (with tower or spire)
C 109	secondary road	P (box)	car park (private)	+	church/chapel (without tower or spire)
	other roads, tracks or drives	🚗	suggested car park for walk or picnic	CH	club house
				F Sta	fire station
	footpaths	✗ 🪑	picnic sites	FB	footbridge
→	route of the main walk and direction	⚡	major viewpoints	F	fountain
		📷	best views on walk	G	garage
				Liby	library
⇒	alternative route described in text	◆ ☎	WC, telephones	MS	milestone
			quarry	Mus	museum
	walk recommended by Jersey Tourism	🏰	castle, fort	PH	pub
				PO	post office
🚌	bus terminus	🏛 *Castle*	prehistoric site	Sch	school
		⊹	other antiquity	T	telephone
🚌	suggested bus stop for walk or picnic	∩	caves	Twr	tower
				TH	town hall

1 ST HELIER HERITAGE

Distance: up to 5mi/8km; 2-3h
Grade: very easy

You will need: stout shoes, credit card (optional!)

How to get there: 🚌 or 🚗 to St Helier (park at Pier Road [18]).

The history of Jersey and its main town of St Helier is vivid and sometimes bloody. The Jersey Tourism office and the Jersey Museum are good places to start learning about this delightful holiday island.

Start out at the (very good) Jersey Tourism information office [1] in the Weighbridge area. Walk through the bus station [2] to the Jersey Museum [3], where you will find paintings, furniture, maritime displays and Victoriana, as well as an entire room devoted to Jersey's famous actress daughter, Lillie Langtry. Serious enquirers are welcome in the Jersey Society library next door.

Come back to Mulcaster Street and cross straight over into Bond Street, to reach the south gate of St Helier Parish Churchyard [4]. The saint was a hermit

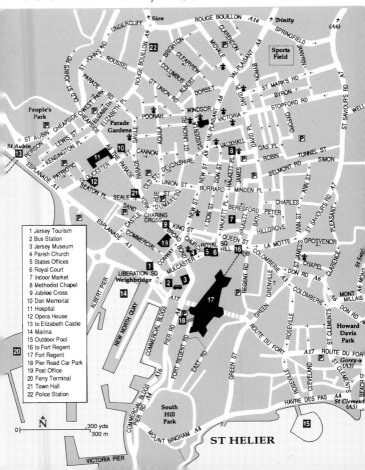

1 Jersey Tourism
2 Bus Station
3 Jersey Museum
4 Parish Church
5 States Offices
6 Royal Court
7 Indoor Market
8 Methodist Chapel
9 Jubilee Cross
10 Don Memorial
11 Hospital
12 Opera House
13 to Elizabeth Castle
14 Marina
15 Outdoor Pool
16 to Fort Regent
17 Fort Regent
18 Pier Road Car Park
19 Post Office
20 Ferry Terminal
21 Town Hall
22 Police Station

ST HELIER

who spent a life of prayer in the tiny hermitage alongside nearby Elizabeth Castle. Walk through the churchyard (and indeed the church) and come to Church Street, once known as La Rue Trousse Cotillon or 'the street of raised petticoats' ... raised just enough for the ladies to cross what was once a filthy, muddy access to the Market Place, now known as Royal Square, which you are about to enter.

On the right are the Jersey Parliament and States Administration Offices [5] and the Royal Court [6], on the left there is an unusual wall-mounted sundial, and at the far end stands an imposing bronze-gilt statue of George II. In the far corner is the Peirson Inn (misspelled in the pub windows). It dates from 1749 but was named after Captain Peirson, who led a stirring victory over the marauding French on 6th January 1781, a day when Royal Square ran deep with blood. This last serious attempt by the French to capture Jersey is recorded in a painting in the Tate Gallery, London, a copy of which hangs in the Royal Court. Just opposite the Peirson, note a fire insurance company mark on the wall of a jeweller's shop. In the early days of fire-fighting, your fire would only be put out by the insuring company if you had paid the premiums beforehand. No plaque? Well, then you had a conflagration, sir.

Leave the square near the pub, then turn right to

reach the pedestrianised shopping zone of King Street/ Queen Street. Turn right, then go left down Halkett Street, to turn into the indoor market [7], opposite the Café de Paris. Leave on the opposite side of the market, so that you come out into Halkett Place. Turn left and walk a short distance to Queen Street. Or ... if it's around lunch-time, and you fancy a traditional fish and chip meal, complete with bread and butter and a cup of tea (other beverages are served, too, including wine), turn right and continue almost to the end of Halkett Place (crossing Burrard Street), until you reach Albert J Ramsbottom's Restaurant. (You'll see the colourful façade of the Methodist Chapel [8] facing you at the end of the street.) If you are a collector, you may like to know that you are now in a part of St Helier that is crammed with small shops, selling antiques, bric-a-brac, craft and off-beat items. From here walk back through Halkett Place to regain Queen Street.

Once back on Queen Street, turn right and walk by all the grand shops as you enter King Street and then Charing Cross. Here you find a granite cross [9] commemorating the Queen's Jubilee in 1977. Note its depiction of twelve aspects of Jersey life, from St Helier's hermitage to a sailing ship, from a milk churn to an ormer (a native shellfish delicacy). The surrounding flower bed is edged with granite blocks taken from

every quarry on the island and stone from the offshore reefs.

Bear right along York Street and into The Parade, packed with gift shops selling everything from kitsch to quality goods. Pass Parade Gardens and an imposing memorial to General Sir George Don [10], with four old guns at its base. He was a well-known Lieutenant Governor of Jersey in the early 19th century.

Turn left into Gloucester Street, passing to the left of a hospital [11] and a nurses' home which was once the Jersey prison (the present jail is on the coast

The indoor market in St Helier displays Jersey's produce at its finest, ranged round a lovely ornamental fountain.

Elizabeth Castle and its causeway: you can walk over to the castle when the tide is out; otherwise there's a ferry journey by amphibious vehicle (Picnic 1).

east of La Corbière). On the left you'll see the Opera House [12], which enjoys a fine summer season.

Gloucester Street leads to the Esplanade, where you turn left. You *could* turn right to get to the causeway [13] to Elizabeth Castle (Picnic 1), which starts almost opposite the Grand Hotel, but you might prefer to save this for a whole morning or afternoon. If you *do* walk over, be sure of the tides. (You can also make the trip in an amphibious 'boat'. The Jersey Tourism office will tell you about the castle, which is well worth an excursion.)

The Esplanade takes you back to Weighbridge. You've now been walking for **1h-1h30min**. If you wish to make a longer circuit, head back to Pier Road. Walk past the rear of the museum, to get improving views over the marina [14] and harbour areas of St Helier. At the point where Pier Road joins the coast road to the east of the island, cross into a pleasant area of parkland with good views east and west, and walk through it to regain the coast road. Drop down to the open-air bathing pool [15] and then, some 300 metres/yards further on, look out for Beach Road on the left. Walk along it and cross the busy Route du Fort into Howard Davis Park, a lovely spacious memorial created in 1937 by a Mr T B Davis, in honour of his soldier son who died in the First World War.

You come out of the park on the opposite side and bear left along Don Road and then Colomberie, to reach the 'train' [16] that takes visitors up to Fort Regent [17] for a small charge (operates early April to end October). At last, you solve the mystery of that huge, strange-looking building which you spotted as you approached the town. Built around an early 19th-century fortress, this is now a vast leisure complex, with everything from swimming to snooker, concert halls, funfair and adventure playground. Much of it is under cover ... paradise, I dare say, for the fractious family on a wet day. From here use the escalator and lift to return to the Pier Road car park [18] in about **3h**.

2 ST BRELADE AND PORTELET COMMON

Distance: 4.5mi/7km; about 2h   See also photograph page 11

Grade: easy, with one short ascent from L'Ouaisné to Portelet

You will need: comfortable shoes, binoculars

How to get there and return: 🚌 14 to St Brelade's Bay and join the circuit at St Brelade's Church, or 🚗 to L'Ouaisné car park.

Short walks

1 L'Ouaisné — St Brelade's Church — L'Ouaisné (2.5mi/4km; 1h; easy). Access as main walk. Follow the main walk for 1h.

2 Portelet Common (1mi/1.75km; 30min; easy). 🚗 to Portelet Common (park nearby, as unobtrusively as possible). Stroll around the common, taking any paths you like. Fine views over the whole of St Brelade's Bay.

S trollers' corner (as I call it) is perfect for early morning or evening rambles of no great length, when the light over the sea is at its most intriguing and the air at its freshest. This walk lasts but a couple of hours; you can make it even shorter by dividing it into two strolls.

Starting at L'Ouaisné car park, head across the sand to St Brelade's Church, tucked picturesquely by the harbourside. Nearby is a fishermen's chapel thought to be of 12th-century origin. Parts of the church are Norman and, in the southeast corner of the churchyard, you'll see the beginning of the shortest sanctuary path (*perquage*) on the island, along which criminals could escape justice centuries ago, if they vowed never to return. In the little harbour shown below note the mooring posts made of tree stumps and, at the back end of this jetty, a flight of steps leading to Le Coleron, once a gun battery, now a viewpoint owned by the National Trust. A path leads from behind the church to Le Beau Port (often signposted as Beauport), an optional detour adding about 40 minutes return: see dashed green lines on the map. This is a quiet, unspoiled location with a

The little harbour at St Brelade

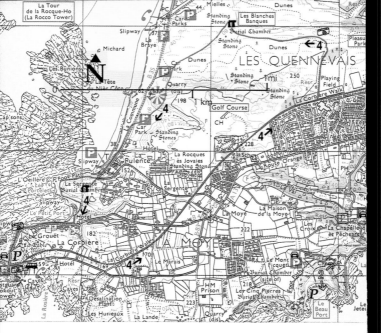

very pretty beach (Picnic 2; see photo page 11).

Return to L'Ouaisné along the promenade and sea-wall which was built as an anti-tank wall by the Germans. At the end of the promenade, climb steps to

L'Ile au Guerdain in Portelet Bay holds the tomb of Philippe Janvrin, a sailor. He died from the plague in 1721, while on a ship returning from France, and he was buried here to minimise the risk of his illness being contracted by islanders. You can reach the island at low tide (see Walk 3).

Le Grouin and ascend the hill either directly or on a gentler path to the right. Then follow a path down to the eastern half of the bay. This crosses private land, but walkers are welcome if they keep to the path. The path passes an old tower and leads back to L'Ouaisné (**1h**).

Portelet Common is not well signposted. To reach it, follow the narrow road east from L'Ouaisné for half a mile/600m, then turn sharp right and take another narrow road running behind the Jersey Holiday Village. From the common you enjoy lovely views over the whole of St Brelade's Bay to the west, as well as L'Ile au Guerdain, the intriguing little island pictured opposite. Visit it on Walk 3, providing the tide is out!

Return from the common along the same roads (**2h**).

3 NOIRMONT, JERSEY VILLAGE AND PORTELET BAY

See map pages 30-31; see also photograph pages 14-15
Distance: 2.75mi/4.5km; 1h20min
Grade: easy, but there is a fairly steep descent to the beach at Portelet Bay, and a corresponding ascent (this can, however, be avoided).
You will need: comfortable shoes or trainers
How to get there and return: 🚌 12 to the Old Portelet Inn (from where you begin by referring to paragraph 4 below), or 🚗 to Noirmont car park, where the walk below begins. Return the same way.
Alternative walk: St Aubin — Noirmont — Jersey Village — St Aubin (5mi/8km; 2h30min; grade as above. 🚌 12, 12a, 14, 15 or 🚗 to St Aubin harbour. Walk south along the harbour, then climb a narrow road, to join the walk described below at the crossroads north of Le Manoir de Noir Mont (picking up the 'Foot and bridle path' mentioned in paragraph 3 on page 33). Return the same way.

This is a fairly short circular walk, but be warned: if you do the complete route, you'll need stamina for the stiff climb from Portelet beach, up what seem to be never-ending steps. (You can, however, enjoy superb views of St Aubin's Bay and Portelet Bay without descending to the beach.) There are no refreshment facilities at Noirmont, apart from an occasional ice-cream van, but en route you'll be able to refresh yourself at the Old Portelet Inn, Janvrin's Restaurant, the beach café at Portelet or the Quarry bar at Jersey Village.

From the car park, **start** by walking back along the road you followed to reach the headland. After some 300 yards/metres turn left onto a footpath which will take you across to a viewpoint from which you can look down over Portelet Bay with L'Ile au Guerdain as its focal point. Above, on the cliff-tops, you'll see the extensive grounds of Jersey Village, a holiday village through which the walk will shortly take you.

The area you are in is covered with footpaths. Take one of your choice back to the road and turn left. When you reach the T-junction (just after passing between farm buildings), turn left again until, after a few minutes, you reach the Portelet car park and bus stop (on your left) and the Old Portelet Inn (set back on your right). *This is where you join the walk if you come by bus.*

Now look for a path on the left just by the car park; it's signposted to Portelet Bay and gives a warning about the number of steps you'll encounter. Set off down the path which, as promised, soon becomes steps. (Or, if you cannot face the descent and subsequent climb, carry straight on, passing Janvrin's Restaurant and the Old Portelet Inn, through a barrier that bars traffic from this narrow road and past a riding stable on your right, until you reach the entrance to Jersey Village. Then pick up the notes in paragraph 3 below, turning right to pass the Bergerac Hotel.)

When you reach the beach (**25min**), take a breather before starting the upward climb. If the tide is safely out (and not on the turn!), you may wish to climb to the top of L'Ile au Guerdain and explore the tower over Janvrin's tomb. Walk to your right along the sand until you reach the beach shop and café. Directly behind the café is a WC and the start of another set of steps that will take you back to the cliff-top. These steps initially bring you back to the holiday village. Turn left onto the main road that runs in front of the residents' accommodation. Pass the main building (the Quarry bar is open to non-residents, and if you need something to refresh you after your climb, it is strategically placed). Jersey Village ('Holiday Village' on the map) occupies what is probably one of the finest sites on the island and, as you walk through the grounds, you enjoy wonderful views over the bay. Follow the road as it curves up through the colourful flower-filled grounds. Just after you pass the children's play area on your right, reach the main exit from the village, joining the road. *This is where those who avoided the steps rejoin the walk.*

Here, turn left and walk past the Bergerac Hotel until you come to a T-junction adjacent to the Portelet Hotel, at which you turn right. (Walk 2 follows this road, to Portelet Common.) Be careful: the road is narrow but there can be a fair amount of traffic. Within a few minutes, reach another junction and again turn right. Shortly, you'll come to a crossroads (**1h**). Here you leave the road and take the pathway (signposted 'Foot and bridle path to Noirmont'). You'll see it on the other side of the junction, on the right. The path briefly passes through woods, then you'll find yourself in semi-moorland, with huge clumps of gorse and broom, a glorious blaze of gold with a heady fragrance, especially in

Broom and gorse weave paths of gold on the way back to Noirmont.

Some of the relics of the Occupation at Noirmont (see also photograph pages 14-15).

May and June. The main path has a netting fence on the left which marks the boundary of the grounds of Le Manoir de Noir Mont, but on your right you'll see dozens of side paths along which you can wander if you are so inclined; they all eventually lead back to the main path, which you can recognise by the fencing.

A few minutes' walking will bring you to more open land, and you will see your destination in the distance. As you approach Noirmont car park, one of the preserved gun emplacements comes into view and, momentarily, you can visualise what the heavily-defended coast of the island looked like during the Second World War. Noirmont (the 'black hill'; Picnic 3) is aptly named: this headland at the western end of St Aubin's Bay is open space dedicated to the memory of all Jersey people who died during World War II.

You'll see two German guns, stark symbols of Jersey's dark days of Occupation. Even more stark is the German bunker built into the headland (see the photograph above), maintained as a museum by the Channel Islands Occupation Society. The 40ft/12m-deep, two-level bunker is open on Thursday evenings during June, July and August and, if you time it appropriately, you could fit in a visit at the end of your walk.

Spend a few more minutes in reflection while looking round the relics, before returning to your car (**1h20min**). If you used the bus and joined the walk at Portelet, continue back to your bus by using the notes in the second and third paragraphs on page 32.

4 THE CORBIÈRE WALK

See map pages 30-31; see also photographs pages 5, 10, 17.

Distance: 8mi/13km; 3h30min   **Grade:** easy

You will need: stout shoes, sunhat, water in hot weather, binoculars

How to get there and return: 🚌 12, 12a, 14, 15 or 🚢 to St Aubin harbour; return the same way.

It's more than 50 years since a steam railway operated from St Helier to St Aubin, along the wide bay, then cutting inland across St Brelade parish for a 3.5mi/6km run to La Corbière lighthouse, one of Jersey's most visited landmarks. The steam romantic's loss is the walker's gain, for the old route makes an excellent, easy walk with refreshments and bus connections at either end. Incidentally, the Jersey Light Railway Society hope that it may be possible to reopen the railway at a future date, so walk *now,* while you have the opportunity!

I have varied the route from the signposted walk (extending the total distance slightly), to give you much finer views and a close look at a sand-dune environment, as well as some prehistoric standing stones. Birdwatchers could find this route a happy twitching-ground, for woodpecker and warbler, wader and finch.

At St Aubin harbour, where the road turns inland, **the start** of the Corbière Walk is well indicated at the entrance to a short tunnel. Follow the walk for about 2mi/3km through pleasant woodland (crossing two roads), until Les Quennevais School is on your left (**50min**). On the right are its playing fields and beyond, the edge of La Moye golf course. Between them is a path: follow it a little way, under pine trees. You emerge with the playing fields on the right and sandy golf links on the left. Ahead is a good view of Jersey airport. Carry on for a few minutes, then turn left across the dunes (near a stile). There is no clear path: just choose the easiest way. This area is known as Les Blanches Banques and is of great interest to botanists who cherish its rare orchids and variety of grasses. It's part of the three-mile stretch of dunes known as Les Mielles.

Ahead is the magnificent sweep of St Ouen's Bay (pronounced One's), and you will see Rocco Tower to the south of it. Look over the lower sandy plain towards the tower, and you should spot a standing stone (menhir) which is your next landfall. Head down from the upper dune system along the easiest route you can find and inspect the stone (with a 'sister' stone and a small burial chamber nearby). Some of Jersey's many

Then (in the early 1900s), passengers alight from a train at the Corbière terminus of the railway line from St Helier ...

prehistoric sites are believed to have been associated with primitive forms of worship.

La Corbière lighthouse now lies south. Head towards it, across the lower dune area. You make easy progress now. Your first target is a car park with steps leading out of it past an old German bunker on the right. You will then look over a second car park: drop down to it and, at the far end, cross the road. Follow the roadside path until you reach a sharp left-hand bend. Here the main path curves right, round the base of a cliff, but you can first climb to the top of the cliff to see La Sergenté, the oldest tomb on the island (3700 BC). It's a private path with permitted access. The lower path (also private with permitted acess) brings you round to Le Petit Port (**2h30min**), a pretty bay offering shelter to a wide variety of birds, especially waders and warblers.

From here it's another 15-20 minutes along the road to La Corbière (Picnic 4), a fine sight at any time but perhaps at its best in a winter southwesterly storm. If the tide is out, you can walk across the causeway to the lighthouse, but watch you don't get caught by the incoming tide!

From the terminus near La Corbière you can catch bus 12, timetable permitting. The main walk continues back to St Aubin: look out for a path on the left, as you walk up the road (it's just opposite the toilets and signposted 'Corbière Walk'). The path will bring you to the old railway station shown below (the platform and one or two other relics still remain). Then just follow the track all the way back to St Aubin (**3h30min**).

... and now. The station still stands, but is today the terminus (or starting point) for walkers, not for trains.

5 LE VAL DE LA MARE

Distance: 5.25mi/8.5km; 3h

Grade: moderate; there are a few steep (though short) sections

You will need: stout shoes, sunhat, water in hot weather

How to get there and return: 🚌 9 (alight at New Road) or 🚗 to the Val de la Mare car park on the A12; return the same way.

Short walk: Circuit of the Val de la Mare Reservoir (2.75mi/4.5km; 1h15min; easy). Access as above. Follow the main walk for 30min. Then climb up the other side of the valley and continue to skirt the reservoir. You will cross a causeway and enjoy fine views to St Ouen's Bay (Picnic 5b). On reaching your outgoing path, follow it back to the bus stop/car park.

This is the most varied of our walks, taking in a lovely reservoir circuit, a section of country park, and a Neolithic burial chamber. It will not seriously challenge experienced walkers, but has one or two steep sections.

Start the walk at the reservoir bus stop/car park on the A12: take the path waymarked to the reservoir (built in the 1960s; **15min**). Bear left here, and follow the waterside path round to the 100ft/30m-high dam and from there descend to the valley floor at the foot of the dam (**30min**). *Those doing the Short walk continue up the other side of the valley, to circle the reservoir.*

Follow the reservoir road seawards, reaching La Rue de le Mare near the Sunset Nurseries. Here turn right for

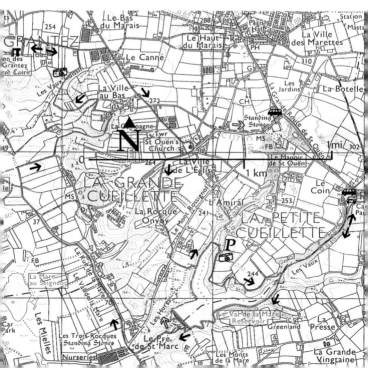

just under 1mi/1.25km, until you see Mont Matthieu, a road on your right. (Those interested in wartime relics might wish to make a short detour some 400 yards/ metres up this road, to the remains of one of a very few wartime bunkers bearing original German Bauhaus-style lettering cast in concrete: GESTEINSBOHR KOMP 77. The bunker is on the right. Allow half an hour extra for this detour, marked in dashed green lines on the map.)

Not far beyond the Mont Matthieu turning, soon after you've drawn level with Kempt Tower off on your left (**1h**), look for a sand extraction area on the right. Immediately after the sand pits is a rutted track, also on the right and, in the distance, you'll see a couple of houses on either side of it, below the hillside. Follow this track; it passes in front of one of the houses and then winds uphill to become the old donkey trail shown opposite, dating from the time when 'vraic' (seaweed) was used by farmers as a natural fertiliser. You pass by a picturesque pond and arrive at La Ville au Bas.

Here, turn left almost immediately. You follow a wider, but still-rough track for a short distance, until you arrive at a spot where a waymarked path comes up from the left (it leads to Picnic 5a at Le Mielle de Morville, just off the map). Ignore this, but join its continuation as it loops round and descends, along the edge of a field, into a valley (Les Vaux Cuissin).

Soon after you reach the valley floor, cross a little wooden bridge over a stream, then climb the other side for more fine views. Soon there are glass-houses over to your right and a high privet hedge alongside you, as

Picnic 5b: Le Val de la Mare Reservoir, with St Ouen's Bay in the distance

The trail, once used by donkeys carrying seaweed, as seen from La Ville au Bas, with the pond referred to in the text on the left.

you reach a metalled road, Le Chemin des Monts. Turn left for about 500 yards/metres, from where the Dolmen des Monts Grantez is accessible across a field on your left. It's one of the more substantial prehistoric graves on the island; uncovered early this century, it yielded several 5,000 year-old skeletons.

Retrace your steps back to the road. Bear right, and keep straight on, past Les Vaux Cuissin, to a road junction. Turn right. There is a view of an old mill on the right at you follow a lane marked 'dead end' and approach St Ouen's Church (pronounced 'One's' and dating from pre-Norman times; **2h10min**). (From here you could walk about half a mile east to St Ouen's Manor crossroads, to pick up bus 9.)

The main walk continues by turning right from the main door of the church. Then take the first left into La Rue de la Campagne, walking past fields still farmed in the strip manner of medieval times. At a road junction, turn right, then very soon bear left on a track signposted to the Val de la Mare Reservoir. Take the left fork in the track and, at a small car park, go through a gate and descend a narrow path to the edge of the reservoir.

Turn left to follow the path round this arm of the reservoir, cross a causeway and climb gently to enjoy splendid views towards St Ouen's Bay, with Jersey airport over to your left. There are seats here, and grassy slopes which make an excellent picnic spot (Picnic 5b). A few minutes further on you reach your outward route; follow it back to the bus stop/car park (**3h**).

6 THE PINNACLE

See map of the north coast on the reverse of the touring map; see also cover photograph

Distance: 3mi/5km; 1h30min   **Grade:** moderate

You will need: stout shoes, binoculars

How to get there and return: You can begin this walk at either Grosnez or L'Etacq. 🚌 8 or 🚗 to the car park at Grosnez; 🚌 12a or car to the car park just below the Lobster Pot hotel and restaurant at Le Grand Etacquerel (the Etacq bus terminus); return the same way.

Witchcraft and pagan rituals have made their mark on Jersey's history, as you may wish to read in appropriate sources (see suggested books on page 6). While researching this book, I exercised my usual traveller's curiosity at most relevant sites, without being turned into a toad or even faintly discomfited. But there *is* something about this windswept cliff-top, with its Nazi detritus, and the claustrophobic amphitheatre cradling The Pinnacle, that disturbs my spiritual tentacles. See what you think. For good measure there's Grosnez 'castle', the ruins of a 14th-century defence against the French who were demonstrably given to looting, pillaging, arson, rape, murder and hamstringing on many a bloodthirsty 'away-day'.

So you tread on interesting soil. **Start out** at either Grosnez or Le Grand Etacquerel. From Grosnez just follow the cliff-top path south, with German observation towers as guide posts. From Le Grand Etacquerel climb the road behind the car park, to pick up the sign-posted path to the cliff-top; you pass a bunker or two.

The 200ft/60m-high Pinnacle rock (Picnic 6) looks benign enough on the approach (**30min** from Grosnez;

A carpet of thrift on a sunny day at Grosnez, but mist is rising from the sea, creating an air of mystery and menace around the castle ruins.

Picnic 6: from the distance, the towering mass of the Pinnacle does not look too formidable. But climb down into the amphitheatre in front of it and it takes on a totally different aspect. Take care not to lose your footing, and do make sure you visit here in the company of others. If you're unsure of your agility on the steep, stony paths, content yourself with admiring it from the cliff-top! (See the cover illustration for a close-up view.)

20min from L'Etacq). Neolithic man once worshipped here, as did the Romans (note the stone formations at the base of the rock; they are the remains of a Gallo-Roman temple). But scramble down a steep path into the amphitheatre. Now the rock looms large in front of you, the cliff seems to crowd in behind you, and there's danger left and right if you stray too far. I was quite happy to regain the cliff path.

There are splendid views along the whole coastline (which is why the Germans built so many towers here) and, over to the right, you'll see Les Landes Racecourse, where there are several meetings during the holiday season. After you have walked from Grosnez to Le Grand Etacquerel (or vice versa), you can vary your return route by taking the path slightly inland (see walking map on the reverse of the touring map). You will skirt the racecourse and pass a rifle range and an airfield for model aircraft. Whichever route you choose, you should be back at your transport in **1h30min**.

While you're in the area and if you want to know more about Jersey's pagan connections, take a look at the Crucible Folklore Museum near L'Etacq.

7 THE NORTH COAST

See map on reverse of the touring map; see also photograph page 16

Distance: up to 15mi/24km; about 8h (beginning at Grosnez). The walk is best done in two days, breaking at Bonne Nuit Bay.

Grade: quite strenuous in places

Equipment: stout shoes or light boots, tide table, binoculars, sun hat, picnic, water

How to get there and return: 🚌 bus links from and to St Helier at various points (see text for details of route numbers); alternatively, start by 🚗 and take a bus back to your parking place.

I have known masochistic walkers capable of devouring the whole of Jersey's coastline (about 40mi/65km) in a single trek. They would start at dawn and return in darkness, in need of nurse, wheelchair and balm ... declaring they had enjoyed their day. But they would have seen nothing, except the path ahead. You can 'do' the whole coast, seeing much more, but perhaps taking a week over it and gaining infinitely more pleasure from your exertions.

I have introduced you to some stretches of the coast in earlier walks, and they all form part of Jersey's maritime character. Other admirable rambles can be made along promenades, for instance between St Helier and St Aubin (3mi/5km; illuminated on summer evenings) or on the flat but atmospheric route skirting St Ouen's Bay on the west coast, where surfers are on the crest of a wave and naturalists are in their element.

But in this 'chapter' we'll look at Jersey's north coast, with its towering cliffs, sea-caves accessible at low tide, wooded valleys, and stunning views over perilous reefs towards Guernsey and the other Channel Islands ... and, at the eastern end, to France on a clear day.

You don't need a mass of directions to follow a coastal path: broadly speaking, if you move too far to one side you'll lose sight of the sea; too far the other way and you'll fall into it. Where the way ahead needs a pointer, you have one, thanks to local signposting.

So I will offer a guide to key stages on the 15mi/24km (approximately) of beautiful coast that stretches between Grosnez in the west (Walk 6) and Rozel in the east (Walk 9). It makes sense to me to divide this stretch into at least two days. Nowhere is it really difficult, and at several points you can escape by bus, take refreshment, or divert temporarily to other attractions.

Take 🚌 8 or 🚗 to Grosnez, to **begin the walk**. Heading east, the first port of call is Plémont (1.5mi/2.5km; **45min**; 🚌 7b, 8; Plémont Candle Craft), with

The waterfall cave at Plémont

lovely views over La Grève au Lanchon beach below the holiday camp. It's worth dropping down the steps to look at the waterfall cave running under the beach café, and the distinctive Needle Rock.

Next is La Grève de Lecq (4mi/6.5km; **2h**; 🚐 9; 19th-century barracks, pub with a waterwheel in the bar, and Cæsar's Palace night club!), another excellent beach to explore and a choice of refreshment options. Climb the path indicated near the old barracks for about 0.6mi/1km, then detour round a shooting range (the route varies depending on whether firing is in progress).

Come to Devil's Hole (6mi/10km; **3h**; 🚐 7; La Mare Vineyards, Butterfly Farm, a decent pub, the Priory), a peculiar cave with a blow-hole through which the sea crashes in rough weather to make a noise like Old Nick himself, so they say. You pass a life-size statue of the Devil rising out of a stagnant pool as you take the path down to the cave (photograph page 16). There's a steepish flight of steps at the end of the path, but the coastal views reward your exertions.

Continue to Le Marrioneux viewpoint, then descend into La Vallée des Mouriers and climb out again for more excellent views. To the north, a mile or two offshore, lie the perilous rocks of Paternoster Reef. Walk 8 also follows this stretch of path, which leads to a superb viewpoint at Sorel but then has to leave the coast to avoid Ronez Quarry. This diversion is well enough signposted. On regaining the path, you'll pass a smaller quarry before coming to a pub on your right (near Picnic 7a) and, indicated left, Wolf's Caves (8mi/13km; **4h**). If you're at all unsound in wind and limb, please don't try this extremely steep descent on zigzag steps! See if you can manage the few steps to your right, into the pub. The hundreds of steps lead to a noted nesting colony of shag and eventually to a rocky gorge where there are sea caves and rock pools. Remember to explore *only* at low tide. You may descend the steps skipping like a mountain goat but rest assured, you will come back feeling like a sack of old bones!

The cliff path runs alongside the pub, coming after another kilometre or so to look over the delightfully-named Bonne Nuit Bay (9km/14.5km; **4h30min**; 🚌 4). Here is a super little beach and a pretty harbour, plus café and a bus stop. I would recommend that you break here for the day, especially if you've 'done' Wolf's Caves. Behind the coast road here, on the hillside, there is a steep but short circular walk with magnificent views, on land owned by Jersey National Trust. If you just wanted to spend half a day at Bonne Nuit, this would make an excellent circuit (2mi/3.5km; 1h15min), or you can tack it onto this coastal segment.

The coast path resumes its way east now, passing a hotel before dividing into a lower and upper path. Either way will suit you, but it goes without saying that the best views are from the higher path. Beyond the headland of La Belle Hougue the paths combine again, leading past Le Petit Port (don't blink or you'll miss it) and through a lovely and equally *petit* bit of woodland, to come to Bouley Bay (12mi/19km; **6h**; 🚌 21; Picnic 7b; Jersey Zoo is also on bus route 21). Once a smugglers' haunt, Bouley is a picturesque bay similar to Bonne Nuit, but bathing is more risky here because of a steeply-shelving beach. Motor sport enthusiasts will know Bouley Bay as the venue of a round of the British hill-climbing championships each summer: the kilometre of winding ascent in about 40 seconds is the target! Take a side-stroll here if you wish, up to Le Jardin d'Olivet, scene of a bloody battle with the French in the 16th century.

The coastal path continues from the Water's Edge Hotel, to come after more splendid seaward views to delightful Rozel (15mi/24km; **7h30min**; 🚌 3; Walk 9). Here, if you arrive in the afternoon, you can partake of a cream tea in one of its little cafés, before boarding your bus.

Magnificent scenery like this continues for mile after mile as you walk along the north coast, and is also a feature of Walk 8.

8 SOREL AND LA VALLEE DES MOURIERS

See map on the reverse of the touring map; see photograph opposite
Distance: 2mi/3km; 1h

Grade: moderate; the cliff path is occasionally rough, and there are short stretches of gradient, sometimes with lengthy stretches of steps.

You will need: stout shoes

How to get there and return: 🚗 car to Sorel (ample parking)
Alternative walk: St John's Church — Sorel — coastal path — St John's Church (5mi/8km; 2h30min; grade as above). 🚌 5 to St John's Church. Follow the C101 and C100 to the viewpoint at Sorel, then continue the main walk, before returning to the church/bus stop.

This short circular walk takes in farm land, a peaceful wooded valley, and a stretch of cliff path with fine views and good picnic spots overlooking the sea.

Park your car in either of the two parks at Sorel, a breezy headland adjacent to the busy Ronez granite quarry. **Start** by walking a few hundred yards/metres back along the road you followed to reach the viewpoint. When you reach the T-junction (with Sorel Farm immediately facing you), turn right. Follow the road round the farm buildings (they will be on your left) and keep with it as it takes a right-hand turn. Now, stay on this road, passing one or two houses and occasional roads and paths joining from the left. Still on the same road, at **15min** pass a junction on your left with a 'Give way' sign and soon start going downhill.

Come to a junction where there is a turning off to the right, and soon after, another to the left; ignore them both. When you reach the bottom of the hill, you will find yourself at a small crossroads with a bus stop (**25min**). Here, turn right, taking the road that runs along the left-hand side of a stream, the start of which may be hidden by weeds and foliage.

Now you come to the best part of the walk. Your route gently descends through the Vallee des Mouriers towards the sea. When the road you are on bends left and sweeps uphill past a cottage on your left, take a track that forks away to the right directly opposite the cottage. Pass a small reservoir on your right (**35min**). Shortly before you reach the sea (there's no beach; just a rocky shelf), look to the right for the coastal path and join it, (Walk 7 also follows this section).

From here on, it's just a matter of following the cliff path which, though narrow in parts, is not hazardous, provided that the ground is dry underfoot. In **1h** (less if you are walking briskly) the path brings you back to Sorel and your car — and plenty of grassy picnic spots.

9 ROUND ST MARTIN'S AND ROZEL

See also photographs pages 2 and 20
Distance: 5mi/8km; 3h
Grade: moderate; after a rainy spell, the woodland paths can be muddy. The path between Rozel and Le Havre de Scez (via the Dolmen du Couperon) is also both stony and rather steep in short stretches.
You will need: stout shoes or walking boots
How to get there and return: 🚌 1b (St Catherine's Bay bus); alight at La Mare, or 🚗 to the car park at La Mare slipway; return the same way.

This delightful inland walk takes you through woodland and along quiet country roads and paths flanked by carpets of wild flowers. It also visits the seaside village of Rozel and the Dolmen du Couperon.

From the tower at La Mare slipway, **start out** by turning left and walking up the road, away from the sea. When you reach the crossroads, bear right along the one-way road marked with a no entry sign (for vehicles). Almost immediately, turn left on a track that leads to Rozel woods. This stony track first takes you past a small private fishing pond which began life as a German-built reservoir during the Occupation. It then leads into Rozel woods (Picnic 9), across two lots of stepping stones and alongside a pretty stream. This is the habitat of birds like the great spotted woodpecker, also the red squirrel, the latter a rare creature now on the British mainland.

Follow the path for about **20min**, ignoring another path which joins it from the left (the old *perquage* or 'sanctuary path' from St Martin's, down which in days gone by villains could legitimately flee the island if they promised never to come back!).

In less than 200 yards/metres, come to a T-junction of paths and go left. The path now climbs fairly steeply out of the woods. After another 400 yards/metres it becomes surfaced with tarmac and bends left, to take you past a farm on your left. As the farm buildings end, turn right. Walk along a lane which passes through farming land. You'll see on your left a huge multi-sided construction surmounted by a lot of mushroom-shaped domes. It looks like some enormous spacecraft that has just landed, but is part of the airport's navigational aids. You are now nearly at St Martin's. A few minutes later, come out into Rue de Belin, where the Methodist Chapel is on your right. Pass the chapel and, within a few yards/metres emerge on the main B38 (**40min**), where you turn right.

After ten minutes you cross a stream (though you may not be able to see any water for all the trees). Five minutes later reach a T-junction and go left. Soon you will have a good view of St Martin's over to the left and, in another 200 yards/metres (near a post box set in a wall), turn right into Rue du Moulin. You'll see the tower shown here, the remains of one of Jersey's oldest windmills. Set in private grounds, it is a fine sight. Follow the road down through a narrow one-way system, dropping into Rozel Valley and turning right to reach Rozel Bay (**1h15min**).

Rozel is a lovely place to linger but, to continue the walk, climb the road, with superb views to your left over the harbour. At the top of the hill, look out for an entrance on your right marked 'Le Saie House'. Immediately beyond this, turn left on a signposted footpath which drops steeply with fine views over Rozel and the inlet of Le Douët de la Mer. The path twists and turns, drops and climbs, reaching Le Couperon, the prehistoric burial site shown opposite (just a few yards/metres to your left; **1h40min**). It is one of only two gallery graves on Jersey. Continue downhill for a few yards/metres, to the end of Rue des Fontenelles. ('Rue' is rather an overstatement here and elsewhere on Jersey, where it describes even the most humble of paths.)

At this point you will see a small car park and a path running off to the left of the main car park. This leads down to Le Havre de Scez (not strictly a harbour, though seaweed for fertilising the land was once collected here), a pleasant and sometimes-deserted beach. You might like to take a short detour to see it. The walk continues on what now becomes a narrow tarmac road, which swings round to the right and starts to climb.

Come to a grassy clearing on the left marked 'Passing

Place', with a 'Jersey National Trust 1936' sign. Here, at the rear of the left-hand side of the clearing, you may spot a rough path. It leads to your next landmark, La Coupe but, unfortunately, it crosses privately-owned land. Pleasant though it would be to leave the road at this point and use a path overlooking the sea, please respect the rights of the landowners and *continue on the road*. Hopefully, this path will be added one day to the list of those which are officially maintained for walkers. The road soon veers quite sharply to the left; about ten minutes later, take the first turning to the left. Follow this road down an increasing gradient until you reach La Coupe (**2h05min**), the promontory shown in the photograph below. There is access to a small beach down a path on the right.

Then climb back up the road until you reach the T-junction. Turn left, following the road as it twists right, then left, as far as a crossroads. Go straight across and, not far beyond a riding centre on your right, turn into a road that forks back to the right (signposted Les Mares). This passes between a few buildings and rapidly becomes a narrow dirt path leading down to Rozel Woods. At the point where it changes to a tarmac surface and becomes walled on both sides, look across to the right for a fine view of Rozel Manor. Continue down the path and come back to the junction where, earlier in the walk, you turned left to climb out of the woods and up to St Martin's. From here, retrace your steps back to the bus stop or car park at La Mare (**3h**).

The Dolmen du Couperon. In the background, beyond Le Havre de Scez beach, is La Coupe, a small headland topped by a little tower.

10 A SHORT STROLL AROUND FLICQUET

See map page 47   **Distance:** 2mi/3km; 1h
Grade: easy, with just a couple of gradients
You will need: comfortable shoes or trainers
How to get there and return: 🚌 1b or 🚗 to St Catherine's Bay
(ample parking); return the same way.

Motorists often like to break their driving with a circular walk of a couple of miles. This one is ideal: there's easy parking at St Catherine's Bay and a convenient café where you can enjoy a Jersey cream tea after your walk. It's little more than a variation on Walk 9, but it is often overlooked by the many people who park at St Catherine's and, wanting a breather, simply stroll to the end of the breakwater and back.

Park in the car park in front of the café (or in one of the spaces overlooking the harbour, between the café and the yacht club). **Start out** by walking back, past the café and WC, along the loop road you took to reach the harbour. In a matter of 200 yards/metres, you'll see the start of a footpath on the right-hand side of the road. Take this path. Almost immediately it divides, with a sign indicating an upper path (left) and lower path (right), both to Flicquet Bay. Choose the path to your right; this lower path takes you along a shady stretch just by the sea. (At the right time of day, you can find a pleasant picnic spot with a seat on this path, as in the setting shown below.) In five minutes or so the path brings you out onto a secluded road, at which you bear right and walk downhill to the quiet little cove at Flicquet, with its ancient defence tower.

This attractive little path takes you beside the sea when you walk from St Catherine's Bay to Flicquet; it makes a pleasant picnic spot.

This unusual house at Flicquet is built in Spanish style.

Pass the tower and continue along the road, which starts to climb gently. Soon you'll come to the pseudo-Spanish style house shown here, a 20th-century folly built beside the road, on your left. The road takes a sharp hairpin bend to pass three sides of this unusual residence, then curves upwards past an attractive row of cottages set back on the right. The flowers surrounding these cottages are a delight if you pass by in spring or summer.

Continue along the road, which is quiet and unlikely to have any traffic, apart from the occasional car trying its luck for a parking space at tiny Flicquet. Pass a bungalow on your left; it appears to be constructed entirely from wooden tiles. At **25min** you reach a road junction: turn left. Walk 9 also follows this short stretch of road, where (at the right time of year) the hedgerow is a mass of colourful flowers, planted by an imaginative resident. Soon pass riding stables on the right and then a road off to Les Mares (where Walk 9 turns off to the right). In another 150 yards/metres, take the road on the left signposted to Flicquet. Pass minor turnings on both sides of the road until, after half a mile/0.75km of gentle downhill gradient, the road takes a sharp turn to the left. Just at the point where it bends, take the track leading downhill to the right.

This track is significantly steeper than the road you have been following. Soon you'll reach a bit of wartime history: two sets of anti-tank barriers which were erected by the German Occupation forces, the sole surviving examples of their type. They consist of lengths of old railway track embedded vertically in the track underfoot, and they're a relic of one of Jersey's long-defunct railways.

When you reach the bottom of the hill, you will find yourself back at the point where you had the option of an upper or lower path to Flicquet. Bear left beside the sea wall and follow the road. Within a couple of minutes you arrive back at the bus stop/car park (**1h**).

11 ST CATHERINE'S TO GOREY

See map page 47
Distance: 3mi/5km; 1h   **Grade:** easy
You will need: stout shoes
How to get there and return:  1b or 🚗 to St Catherine's Bay (park near the café close to the end of the breakwater; you'll always find a parking space somewhere here). Return on 🚌 1, 1a, or 1b from Gorey Pier, back to St Helier or to your car at St Catherine's Bay.

S hort though it is, this walk packs a variety of scenery into a few leisurely miles along the east coast. It starts at St Catherine's breakwater, a 250ft/800m-long granite structure built in the mid-1800s as the start of what was to have been a major harbour. However, the Admiralty realised before completing the project that it would be hopelessly silted up most of the time, so just finished the breakwater to save face. It's about a mile out and back, if you wish to walk it first.

Start out by walking back along the road you took to reach St Catherine's Bay (use the path beside the road). Pass La Mare slipway and tower (Walk 9) and two picnic areas with barbecues (Picnic 11a). Then come to a second, 18th-century defence tower on a short breakwater at Archirondel. Immediately beyond it is Archirondel Beach (**30min**): not too crowded, it makes a fine picnic spot, especially on a warm, clear early evening.

The gorgeous sweep of Gorey Bay, seen from the castle at the top of Mont Orgueil. (Notice that the large-scale walking map uses the old spelling of 'Gouray' throughout.)

About halfway round the bay, at the back of the beach, climb some steps and follow a short path through a small field of wild flowers to the coast road and the hotel Les Arches. Turn right on the road (or go left for Picnic 11b). Almost immediately, go left on Rue du Puchots, climbing behind the hotel. On coming to a T-junction, turn left. Within a few hundred yards/ metres, you overlook Anne Port Farm on your left. Take the first (very narrow) lane on your right, to pass the farm. Just beyond it, go left for a few yards/metres: you come to a footpath on the right, signposted to the Dolmen de Faldouët. This 50ft/15m-long prehistoric passage grave (**50min**) has a capstone reckoned to weigh over 20 tonnes. The site is also rumoured to have a more recent association with occult ceremonies.

Return to the road and bear right for some 200 yards/ metres, to a distinct U-bend. The second opening on the bend carries a 'no through road' sign. Walk along it briefly, to get some marvellous views over Gorey Bay towards Mont Orgeuil Castle. If you want to visit the castle, take the one-way road on your left: you come out almost opposite it, on the coast road. Or turn right, to find a footpath into Gorey village (also worth a visit). In either case, your bus leaves from Gorey Pier (**1h**).

12 GREEN ISLAND TO GOREY BAY

See photographs pages 13 and 52-53
Distance: 5mi/8km; 2h
Grade: very easy, but sand conditions can vary
You will need: stout shoes, tide table
How to get there and return: 🚌 1 or 🚗 to Green Island; return by 🚌 1 from Gorey Pier, to Green Island or St Helier.

Green Island, a couple of miles out of St Helier on the east coast road, is a splendid place at low tide for messing about among rock pools and generally enjoying a stretch of beach where there's room for everyone. Connoisseurs of Jersey's prehistoric sites might like to note that a burial ground was excavated on its summit 80 years ago, and the bits are displayed at La Hougue Bie (see Walk 15). It was here that witches gathered centuries ago on Rocque Berg, a very striking lump of granite. It is now on a private driveway and only visible if you walk round the road a little way and have a quick look at it from the gate.

For a very bracing stroll to Gorey (Gouray on the map), **set off** from Green Island along the beach at low or on an ebb tide, otherwise you'll not get round Le Nez, the headland just east of the island. Once round Le Nez, your direction is obvious. Look at the seaward view if the tide is well out — positively lunar! Imagine how many vessels came to grief on those amazing reefs in days of yore. The sea recedes up to two miles here, and you can walk that far out. But *beware*. On the turn, the sea races in through the rocks; you could very easily be stranded, with fatal consequences. Be *absolutely* sure of your timing if you want to explore. *You have been warned.*

About **20min** along the beach (which may be shingly and soft here), you'll come to Le Hocq slipway and 18th-century defence tower, used now by radio enthusiasts. From here the going is quite adequate as far as the southeast corner of Jersey, La Rocque harbour (**1h**). Climb the steps in the sea wall here, and walk round the promenade (notice the splendidly Gothic-looking

house with adjacent defence tower, shown on page 13). The invading French landed here prior to the Battle of Jersey (see the St Helier walk on page 25).

Beyond the harbour take to the beach again, observing the four defence towers of similar design, now incorporated into 'desirable residences'. Beyond the fourth tower, climb steps in the sea wall and follow the promenade to Grouville Common (La Commune de Gouray on the map). This is a lovely stretch underfoot, but note that you are on the edge of the Royal Jersey Golf Club links. The name may be regal, but some stray shots along here can have a very common touch. At the far end of the common, regain the beach. Then climb Gorey village slipway and continue to Gorey pier and your bus stop (**2h**).

13 THE GERMAN UNDERGROUND MILITARY HOSPITAL

Distance: 4mi/6.5km; 2h

Grade: easy

You will need: stout shoes

How to get there and return: 🚌 8a or 🚗 to the German Underground Military Hospital; return by 🚌 8a from the Victoria Hotel, either to St Helier or back to the Underground Hospital.

First-time visitors to Jersey are often surprised to discover the extent and the legacy of the five-year Occupation (1940-45). The story is no more vividly told than at the Underground Military Hospital, a massive tunnel complex built when the Germans entrenched themselves in the Channel Islands, believing them to be stepping stones to a full invasion of the UK. Hitler turned Jersey into a fortress, with gun positions and bunkers located throughout the island, especially on the coast. A visit to the hospital will amaze you. The Führer never felt the island sunshine himself, but his command HQ was about a mile away from the hospital, where the 'Living Legend' now stands. This major tourist attraction (included in the walk) offers free entertainments, as well as a paid-admission 25-minute audio-visual history of Jersey.

Begin at the hospital bus stop. Walk up Mont du Rocher, with a view to the museum entrance on your right. A minute or two later, follow the road as it makes a near-90° turn left, and come to a T-junction with Rue de la Ville au Bas. Turn left again, then go right, gently

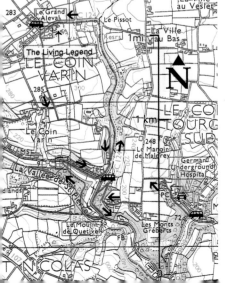

descending to the main road (**30min**) near the Victoria Hotel. Turn left on the road; note that there is no roadside path here, and this road can be quite busy, so take care and walk facing the traffic, for safety's sake.

Soon you reach the Moulin de Quetivel, a historic mill now owned by the Jersey National Trust

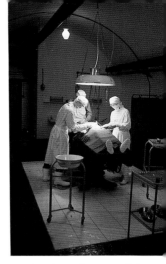

One of the sights that will linger in your memory if you visit the German Underground Military Hospital. The hospital was constructed by forced labour during the war years and remains exactly as it was when the occupying forces left. Tableaux like this one vividly bring to life the incredible achievement of the architect and of the slaves who worked in appalling conditions to complete the project, which in the end was never used in a state of siege or battle, as had been intended.

(open Tuesdays, Wednesdays and Thursdays only). From the car park behind the mill, take the very attractive woodland path; it gives you a taste of St Peter's Valley, as you descend to the main road by a duck pond. Turn right on the road, to come back to the Victoria Hotel (**50min**).

Now bear left into the road signposted to the Living Legend. Almost immediately, on the left, you'll see a tunnel entrance (alongside a cottage). This is now Jersey's principal mushroom farm, though it is not open to the public. Walk on the path at the edge of the road for about 0.6mi/1km: you'll see more tunnel entrances on both sides of the road, most of them overgrown. This whole area is honeycombed with underground reminders of the Occupation.

Turn left on Le Pissot, to reach the Living Legend (**1h25min**), a theme park which opened in 1992. The nerve centre for the Occupation stands in the grounds, now incorporated into the park's buildings. In those days the command HQ was disguised as simple cottages; today it is used as a store and hidden behind shops — not open to the public. You can catch bus 8a here, back to St Helier or the hospital, but the walk continues by turning left just beyond the Living Legend, onto a very quiet road. Keep on until the road makes a sharp turn left and zigzags downhill, back to the tunnel entrance at the mushroom farm.

Catch bus 8a from the Victoria Hotel (**2h**); it calls at the hospital before returning to St Helier. Or retrace your outgoing route back to the car park/bus stop at the hospital itself (add 1mi/1.5km; 30min).

14 GOREY VILLAGE AND QUEEN'S VALLEY

See map page 47

Distance: 4mi/7km; 1h55min

Grade: quite easy

You will need: stout shoes (the reservoir paths are loose grit)

How to get there and return: 🚌 1, 1a or 1b to the terminus at Gorey ('Gouray' on the walking map), or 🚗 to Gorey; return the same way.

Short walk: Queen's Valley Reservoir circuit (2mi/3km; 45min; easy). Walk the perimeter of the lake, possibly using the causeway to cross from one side to the other and achieve a figure-of-eight. 🚌 3a to Queen's Valley (St Saviour's Hospital) or by 🚗 (park at the St Saviour's Hospital end of the reservoir, or at the southern end).

If choosing a walk to feature another of Jersey's reservoirs, many people would immediately think of the aptly-named Waterworks Valley in St Lawrence, where there are several modestly-sized reservoirs strung out alongside the C118 north of Millbrook.

However, Jersey's newest reservoir, resulting from the flooding of Queen's Valley, in my view makes a far more enjoyable walk, because you can get around the entire lake on mainly-level paths, encountering no traffic whatever. I suggest a route that starts at Gorey (Gouray on the map), because this extends the duration of the walk to a respectable two hours, but motorists who want a shorter circular walk can park at either end of the reservoir (see Short walk).

From the bus terminus at Gorey, cross the road and **start out** by walking up the B28 (St Martin's) road out of the village. You have well over half a mile/1.2km to walk on a road that can be fairly busy, but bear with me and keep an eye on the traffic. As you pass the church on your right, the road climbs and curves to the right. This is the least interesting part of the walk, but do look out for the magnificent sunflowers, wrought in metal, which decorate gates at the entrance to a drive on the left side of the road some **15min** after leaving Gorey.

In **25min** come to a road junction where the B28 joins the road you are on becomes the B30, and the B28 turns to the left. Follow the B28 to the left; it is signposted to La Hougue Bie. (Or, if you want some refreshment after the climb up from Gorey, continue for another 200 yards/metres on the B30, to reach a huge undercover garden centre with a restaurant serving both snacks and full-scale meals.)

Some 15 minutes along the B28 (**40min**) come to the northern entrance to the Queen's Valley Reservoir. Here you have the option of walking along whichever

View from the path on the eastern shore of the lake (near Picnic 14)

side of the lake you prefer. I describe the path to your left, running along the eastern side.

Within ten minutes come to a causeway; not far beyond it, there is a grassy picnic area at the left of the path (Picnic 14; see photograph above), where you can take a break and enjoy the view. Continue along the path, which now takes you through a pleasant tree-lined stretch, eventually to reach the dam and overflow tower at the southern end of the lake, which is just under a mile from the north end of the reservoir (**1h**).

Descend a steep winding path with steps and pass the water company's pumping station, to reach Le Chemin des Maltières. Here turn left, passing the Mill Pottery. Ignore a turning that forks back on your left; keep straight along. After ten minutes the road bends sharply to the right and then, almost immediately, it heads left again. Now you'll enjoy fine views of Mont Orgueil Castle in the distance. At **1h25min** come to La Rue Horman and turn right. Within a couple of minutes, you will see the sign for the Jersey Pottery on your left. There is no admission charge, and this pottery is well worth a visit at some point during your stay; it incorporates an excellent restaurant.

Reaching the end of the road, turn left into a road marked with a 'no entry' sign, to reach the main street of Gorey village. It's a pleasantly picturesque area with a few shops and a post office. Continue along the road; it takes you back to the lower end of the B30, near where the walk began. Drop down into Gorey village to reach your bus or car in under **2h**.

15 LA HOUGUE BIE

Distance: 3.5mi/5.5km; 1h15min

Grade: very easy

You will need: stout shoes

How to get there and return: 🚌 3a or 20 or 🚗 to La Hougue Bie; return the same way.

Short walk: La Hougue Bie — La Franche Ville — La Hougue Bie (2mi/4km; 55min; very easy; access as above). Follow the main walk to La Franche Ville (35min), then use the notes at the foot of page 61 to shorten the circuit back to La Hougue Bie.

I would usually apologise for suggesting a walk which stays predominantly on metalled roads, but in this case I won't. Not only do these lanes see little traffic, but they reveal a few Jersey peculiarities. And you wouldn't want to miss those, would you?

Start out at the fascinating site of La Hougue Bie (Picnic 15). Its history goes back to Neolithic times, but became more colourful with the passage of the years. The centre of attention here is a 40ft/12m-high mound, excavated only during this century, revealing a burial chamber which you can inspect by stooping along a narrow passage for some 50 feet/15 metres.

On top of the mound are two chapels of 12th- and 16th-century origin. You can learn all about them in the information centre, which has a useful book section and modest refreshment facilities. There's display of agricultural history at La Hougue Bie too, as well as an archaeological museum, a geology display, and a German regimental headquarters bunker. In short, much to see before you start (or after you finish) the walk.

Coming out of La Hougue Bie, turn right and then right again at the *second* crossroads (under **10min**). You

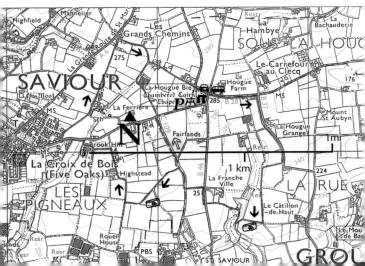

An old Jersey custom: 'marriage stones', built into the homes of newlyweds. They are to be found all over the island, but those illustrated above can be seen on the short version of this walk.

pass the magnificent house and driveway of La Hougue Grange, on your left. No more than ten minutes later, look out for a lane on your right, just before the road makes a 90° turn left. Head along this lane and bear sharp left. Continue for ten minutes, until you can bear right on another lane. Along here you'll start getting magnificent views towards Grouville Bay. Drop down into a small valley and climb gently out of it. Come to a road and turn right, alongside La Franche Ville, which has the finest country brick wall you'll see anywhere.

Where the wall ends, turn left on a short stretch of untarred road. Then turn right and quickly left (**35min**). *The Short walk keeps straight ahead here; see footnote below.*

Keep right where this lane forks, to gain a view over St Clement's Bay. Come to a T-junction and turn right, passing Highstead on the left. Bear left beyond it. After a quick succession of right, left and right turns, come to Prince's Tower Road. Turn left here and continue for a few minutes, then go right into La Rue des Friquettes. You pass St Michael's Preparatory School on the right and soon see La Hougue Bie to the right.

At the next junction, come upon a Methodist church and turn right on a road. To see the marriage stones shown above (they are on the Short walk route), bear right for a few minutes at the next junction: the first is set beside a gate on your right; the second into a wall on your left. Then return to this road, pass La Commune (a three-storey house, noted as an early producer of Jersey cider), and regain La Hougue Bie (**1h15min**).

*For the Short walk, keep ahead here, to a crossroads. Go straight over on a road which eventually descends gently and turns to the right. Now look out on your right for a wall into which is set the 'marriage stone' shown above right. Further along, on your left, beside a gate, is the stone shown above left. Notice, too, the open brook beside the road: most brooks on Jersey are covered over, so that motorists don't bumble into them... Continue along the road to a right turn and head back past La Commune to La Hougue Bie.

BUSES AND INTER-ISLAND TRANSPORT

BUSES

Jersey is well served for bus routes; if you are not hiring a car, you will still be able to get within a mile of virtually any part of the island by one of the many routes operated by the carriers, JMT.

Because the services are so numerous, it is not possible to print full timetables in this guide. Instead, various destinations are shown and the principal route number(s) serving them. The listing includes not only the starting point for all the walks, but some of the island's tourist attractions as well. At the right the *approximate frequency* of services is indicated by the average time between buses on weekdays and Sundays. Note that services are often more frequent between 9am and mid-morning, and again from mid-afternoon until about 6pm. **Note also:** The approximate frequencies shown below are for summer services (mid-May to early October). At other times of the year, be sure to obtain the winter timetable, which is much restricted.

Where the service is so irregular that reference to the up-to-date JMT timetable is *essential,* no frequency is given; you must *refer* to the timetables. You should in any case obtain an up-to-date timetable booklet from the Weighbridge bus station in St Helier, which is the departure point for all services: for some of the destinations, you will find the timetable shows alternative services which provide additional options.

Although a few bus stops are marked by signposts, most are indicated by markings on the road surface. Always wait at an indicated bus stop: *drivers will not pick up passengers at intermediate points.*

On bank holidays, the Sunday bus service operates.

Destination	Route(s)	Approximate frequency	
		Weekdays	*Sundays*
Airport	15	20min	30min
Bonne Nuit Bay	4	1h30min	none
Bouley Bay	21	2h	none
Bunker Museum, St Peter's	9	1h	1h30min
Butterfly Farm	7	1h	none
Candlecraft, Plémont	8	2h	*refer*
Carnation Farm			
(Haute Tombette)	7	1h	none
Carnation Farm (Retreat)	7	1h	none
Château Plaisir	12a	1h	2h
Corbière, La	12	1h15min	2h
Devil's Hole	7	1h	none
Etacq, L'/Le Grand Etacquerel	12a	1h	2h

		Weekdays	Sundays
Fantastic Tropical Gardens	8a	30min	1h
German Underground Military Hospital	8a	30min	1h
Gold Centre	12a	1h	2h
Gorey and the castle	1, 1a, 1b	15min	30min
Green Island	1	30min	45min
Grève de Lecq, La	9	1h	1h30min
Grosnez	8	2h	none
Hougue Bie, La	3a, 20	1h	2h
Jersey Pottery, Gorey	1, 1a, 1b	15min	30min
Landes Racecourse, Les	8	2h	*refer*
Living Legend, The	8a	30min	1h
Micro World	12a	1h	2h
Mielle de Morville, Le	12a	1h	2h
Old Portelet Inn	12	1h30min	2h
Pallot Steam Museum	5	1h	2h
Plémont	7b, 8	2h	*refer*
Portelet Bay	12	1h30min	2h
Queen's Valley (St Saviour's Hospital)	3a	1h	2h
Rozel Bay	3	1h	2h
St Aubin	12, 12a, 14, 15	10-15min	10-15min
St Brelade's Bay	12, 14	30min	1h
St Catherine's Bay	1b	*refer*	none
St John's Church	5	1h	2h
St Mary's Church	7, 7b	1h	*refer*
St Ouen's Bay	12a	1h	2h
St Ouen's Parish Hall	8, 9	1h	1h30min
St Peter's Village	9	1h	1h30min
St Saviour's Hospital	*see Queen's Valley*		
Sorel	*see St John's Church*		
Trinity Church	4	2h	none
Val de la Mare, Le (New Road)	9	1h	1h30min
Zoo	3, 3b, 21, 23	30min	1h

TRANSPORT TO OTHER ISLANDS (OR FRANCE)

You can travel by sea to Guernsey, Sark or Alderney for a day trip, or you can just as easily visit France, which is only a few miles away. To visit the tiny island of Herm, just off Guernsey, you would have to travel to Guernsey and then catch one of the regular ferries.

Since services vary greatly according to the time of year, I recommend that if you are interested in getting away from the island during your visit, you check times at the tourist offices or at the operators' offices on St Helier waterfront. Trips by air (rather more expensive!) are also available: get details from travel agents or the airport.

If you plan to visit France, do remember to take your passport; it will be needed.

✸ Index

Geographical names comprise the only entries in this Index. For other entries, see Contents, page 3. A page number in *italic type* indicates a map; a page number in **bold type** indicates a photograph. Both of these may be in addition to a text reference on the same page. 'TM' refers to the walking map on the reverse of the touring map. See also bus timetable index on page 62.

Anne Port 11, 20, *47*
Archirondel 11, 20, *47*, 52
Beau Port, Le 9, **11**, 15, *30-1*
Belle Hougue, La 44, *TM*
Blanches Banques, Les *30-1*, 35
Bonne Nuit Bay 42, 44, 62, *TM*
Bouley Bay 11, 18, 19, 44, 62, *TM*
Coleron, Le 29
Corbière, La 10, 14, 15, **17**, *30-1*, **36**, 62
Corbière Walk **5**, 22, *30-1*, 35, **36**
Coupe, La 47, **49**
Couperon, Dolmen du *47*, 48, **49**
Croc, Le 21
Dannemarche Reservoir, Le 17
Devil's Hole 14, **16**, 17, 43, 62, *TM*
Douët de la Mer *47*, 48
Elizabeth Castle 9
Etacq, L' 10, 14, 16, 40, 41, 62, *TM*
Faldouët, Dolmen de 20, *47*, 53
Flicquet *47*, **50**, **51**
German Underground Military Hospital 14, 17, *56*, **57**, 62
Gorey (Gouray) 20, 23, 53, *47*, 52, *54-5*, 58, 59, 62
    Bay and Pier *47*, **52-3**, *54-5*, 62
Grand Etacquerel, Le 10, 16, 40, 41, 62, *TM*
Green Island 18, 21, *54-5*, 63
Grève au Lanchon, La 43, *TM*
Grève de Lecq, La 14, 16, 42, 43, 62, *TM*
Grosnez (Gros Nez) 14, 16, **40**, 41, 42, 63, *TM*
Grouville Common *54-5*
Havre de Scez, Le *47*, 48
Hocq, Le 21, *54-5*
Hougue Bie, La 11, 18, 20, *60*, 61, 63
Ile au Guerdain, L' **30**, *30-1*, 32, 33
Jersey (Holiday) Village *30-1*, 32, 33
Jersey Zoo 18, **19**, 63, *TM*
Kempt Tower 11, 15, 38
Landes, Les 41, 63, *TM*
Living Legend, The 15, *56*, 57, 63
Macpela Cemetery 18
Mare slipway, La 11, 46, *47*
Marrioneux, Le 43, *TM*
Mielle de Morville, Le 10, 16, 63
Mielles, Les **10**, 22, 35
Millbrook 14, 17
Mont Orgueil 18, 20, *47*, **52-3**
    Castle *47*, **52-3**, 59

Monts Grantez, Dolmen des 39
Moulin de Quetivel, Le 17, *56*
Nez, Le *54-5*
Noirmont 10, **14-15**, *30-1*, 32, **33**, **34**
North coast path 22, 40, 42-44, *TM*
Pallot Steam Museum **18**, 63
Petit Port, Le *30-1*, 36, 44, *TM*
Pinnacle, The 10, 40, **41**, *TM*, **cover**
Plémont 16, 42, **43**, 63, *TM*
Portelet, Le 14, *30-1*, 32, 34
    Bay **30**, *30-1*, 32, 34, 63
    Common 29, *30-1*,
Ouaisné, L' 29, *30-1*,
Queen's Valley Reservoir 11, 21, *47*, 58, **59**, 63
Rocco Tower *30-1*, 35
Rocque, La **13**, 18, 21, *54-5*
Ronez 10, 43, *47*, *TM*
Rozel 11, 18, 19, 42, 44, 46, *47*, 49, 63, *TM*
    Bay *47*, 48, 63, *TM*
    Moulin de *47*, **48**
    Woods **2**, 11, **20**, 46, *47*, *TM*
St Aubin 14, 23, *30-1*, 35, 63
St Brelade 9, **29**, *30-1*
    St Brelade's Bay 15, **29**, *30-1*, 63
St Catherine's Bay and Breakwater 18, 19, *47*, **50**, 52, 63
St Clement 21, *54-5*
St Helier 9, 14, 17, 18, 25, **26-7**, 28, 62-3
    town plan *25*
St Lawrence 14, 17
St Martin's 46, *47*
St Mary's 14, 63
St Ouen's *37*, 39, 63
    Bay 10, 15, *30-1*, 35, 38, 63
St Peter's Valley *56*, 57
St Saviour's Hospital 11, 20, *47*, 58, 63
Samares Manor 21
Sergenté, La *30-1*, 36
Sion 18
Sorel 43, 45, 63, *TM*
Trinity 18, 63
Val de la Mare, Le 10, 16, *37*, **38**, 63
Vallée des Mouriers, La 43, 45, *TM*
Vaux Cuissin, Les *37*, 38, 39
Ville au Bas, La **39**
Waterworks Valley 17
Wolf's Caves 43, *TM*